CONTE

OXFORDSHIRE:- LOCATIONS OF THE 24 ROUTES

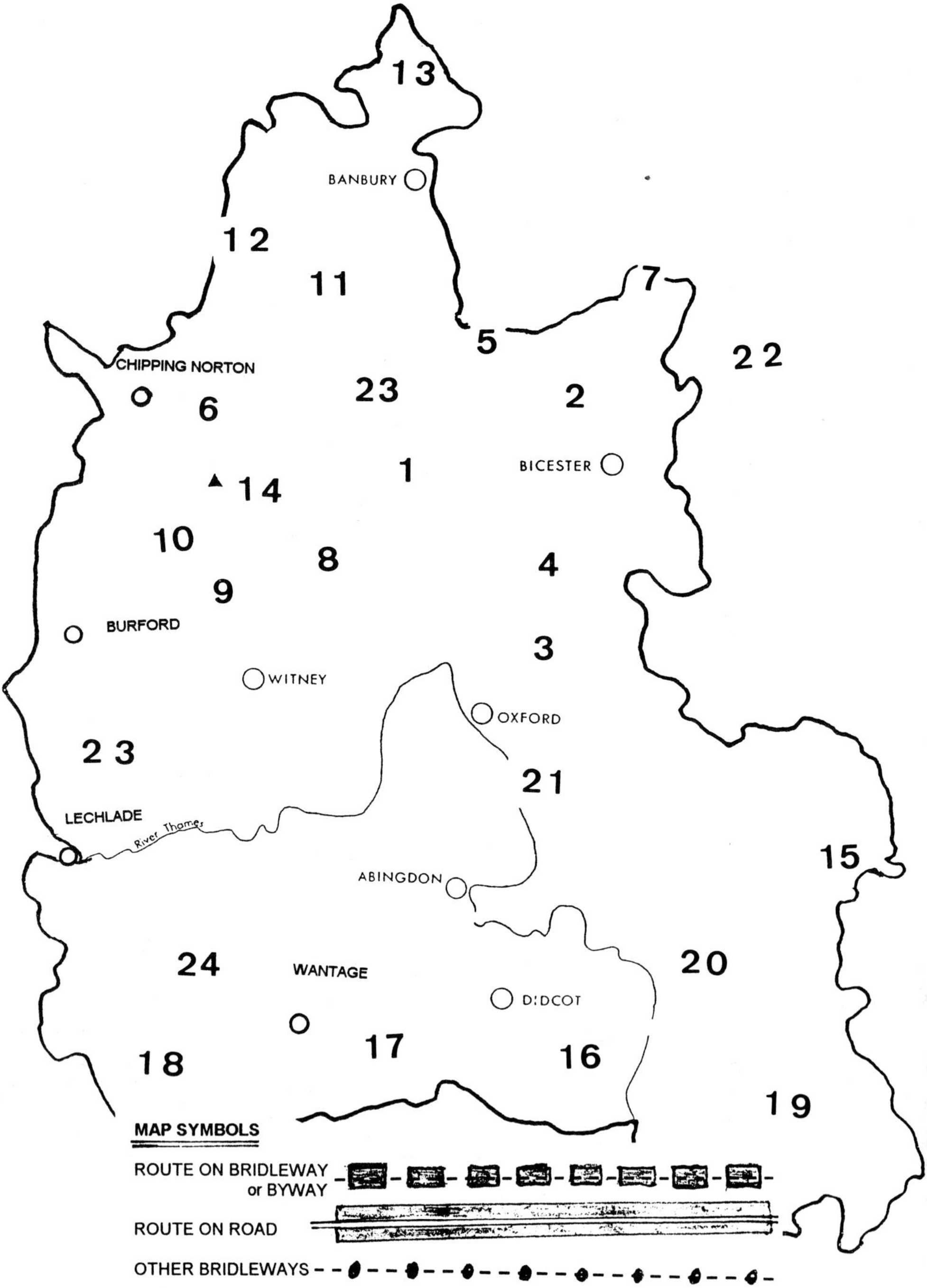

PREFACE

The numbers of riders and drivers have been steadily increasing over the years so safer access routes and bridleways are of paramount importance.

Rights of way and access have been close to my heart for a long time, as I was Oxfordshire County British Horse Society Chairman for nearly ten years, County and Regional Bridleways Officer before that and also Assistant Area Commissioner for the British Driving Society.

This book of rides and drives on bridleways and byways has been the dedicated hard work of Brian Wilson and his trusty steed "Tuftey", who have ridden all the routes twice if not three times, so that we can be sure that they are as accurate as possible.

It shows everyone that there is a surprisingly large number of excellent routes through varied countryside, lush river valleys, open chalk downland and beautiful Cotswold villages with very hospitable watering holes, both for horse and the inner person.

All proceeds from the sale of this book are being donated to Riding for the Disabled in Oxfordshire. We all know the joy of a pair of ears rotating in front of us, listening to our voice and all that is going on around us. How much more wonderful if, for any reason, your mobility is limited until you are with a horse.

Do go out and enjoy the Oxfordshire countryside with your horse.

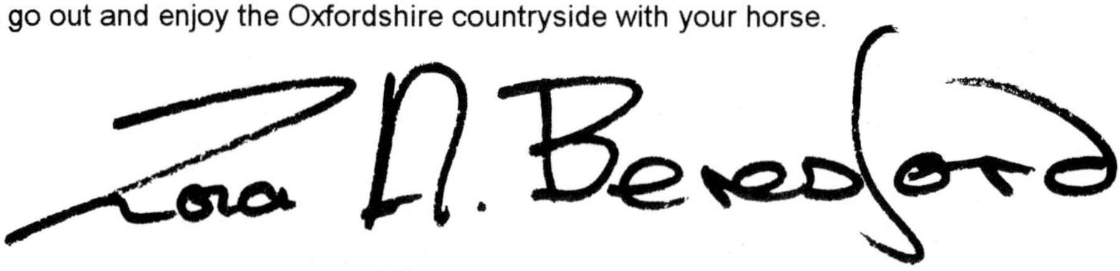

Zoia A. Beresford-Soimenow, Dip. Arch. (Oxford)
Union Hall, Brechfa, Carmarthen, Dyfed SA32 7RA[1]

GOING TO THE DERBY OR TO GRETNA GREEN.

ACKNOWLEDGEMENTS

Many organisations and individuals have given time, expert information or other material help towards this publication. The author is especially grateful to the following:-

- Oxfordshire County Council (O.C.C.) Rights of Way, Highways and Road Safety Departments have examined the routes in draft. Roadside signposting of paths has been extensive and way-marking is now being undertaken throughout the County. The O.C.C. Department of Leisure and Arts has itself published two route descriptions for horse riders ("The Judges Ride" and the "Ewelme Britwell Salome, Cuxham and Pyrton Ride") and six circular routes for cyclists ("The Oxfordshire Cycleway").
- Buckinghamshire County Council (B.C.C.) Officials have made useful comments and published six horse and mountain bike rides, including "Westbury Circular Ride"
- West Oxfordshire District Council and Carterton Town Council have published "Carterton and Villages - Town & Country Rides for horses and mountain bikes".
- The Country Landowners Association (C.L.A.) and the National Farmers Union (N.F.U.) gave their full cooperation and circulated in 1994 and 1995 draft copies of individual route descriptions and maps to their members or their agents for comment, whilst the Ramblers Association (R.A.) also sent helpful comments.
- The National Trust (N.T.) has provided a number of new bridleways specifically to separate horse from vehicular traffic on the Coleshill Park Estate and near the Uffington White Horse. The Lord Saye and Sele has kindly provided a "permissive" bridleway on the Broughton Estate near Banbury.
- The BHS and BDS (British Horse & Driving Societies). Mrs. Zoia Beresford, Chairman of the Oxfordshire Committees of both organisations until her retirement in 1995 gave enormous support. Brenda Wickham, Regional Bridleways Officer and Liz Crossley, former County Bridleways Officer, conceived "*Waylands Way*" as a long distance route. Liz Crossley recruited four District Bridleways Officers, inspired other riders to explore a variety of routes in Oxfordshire (including Chris & Ann Jones, Jane Lewis *nee* Humphries, June Grimston, Vic Mace, Peter Handley, Sir Adam Butler and Jonathan Targett) or to conduct surveys of bridleways in the BHS *"1991 Year of the Arrow"* project (Pat McEwan, Margaret Beadle, Marie Webster, Belinda Thompson, Anna Baness, and Caroline Young).
- Comments from individual members of local hunts, pony clubs, riding schools and riding clubs and many other friends have led to substantial improvements.
- Diedre Fallowes & Harriet Howard ensured liaison over the carriage drives.
- Margaret Cochrane, Tony Peet, Jill Webb, Roy Kinch and Carolyn Henman "proved" several of the routes. Carolyn also did much initial mapping and route measuring as well as a good deal of exploration in foul and fine weather on her coloured cob "*James*".
- Bill Kelly supported this work and loaned his home bred TB "*Horwood Lad*" (placed at Windsor over 6 furlongs as a two y.o.), alias "*Tuftey*", to "develop and prove" all the routes, and to explore many others, in thirty months of all-weather riding.
- Ken Messer provided four original drawings, Allan Fallowes took the photographs.
- Messers B.T.Batsford Ltd. permitted use of material from "Travel in England" by Thomas Burke, 1942. The Countryside Commission authorised reproduction of illustrations by Chris Masters from "Out in the Country", 1992.
- Jill Webb proof read, spotting many errors and inconsistencies.
- Many farmers, publicans, riding schools, riding clubs and BHS Members throughout the county kindly provided safe horsebox parking, invaluable local knowledge, much hospitality and occasionally their own company.

INTRODUCTION

1. Purpose.

This booklet, with descriptions and route maps, has three aims:-

(a) to encourage safe, enjoyable and responsible riding by making optimum use of public bridleways, byways and quiet roads with good verges;

(b) to encourage riders to experience Oxfordshire, not only as landscape but also as a workplace, by fostering harmony and mutual respect between the public with their legitimate desires for leisure-time access and the rural community of farmers and landowners with a legitimate need to derive a livelihood by efficient, commercial land management; and

(c) to raise funds for the charity R.D.A. whose volunteers in fifteen local groups in the county give so much pleasure to physically or mentally disabled children and adults and much support and relief to their carers.

2. Definitions.

Public footpaths, bridleways and byways are "*highways*" in law and are "*paths or routes over which members of the public have legal 'rights of way' i.e. a right of passage for passing, repassing and other purposes reasonably incidental to such movements*" (e.g. to rest or picnic but not to roam off the route; to take photographs but not to take game etc.). "Highways" include all public roads (HA 80 ; Highways Act 1980).

Although disuse of a private path can constitute evidence of abandonment, a public right of way, by whatever means it came into existence (enclosure, tithe etc.), cannot be extinguished by disuse but only by statutory provision.

"*Once a highway, always a highway*".

Use of a public right of way depends upon its highway "status" as follows:-

a) footpaths:- "*a right of passage on foot only*";

b) bridleway:- "*a right of passage on foot, on or leading a horse (donkey or mule), possibly also droving, and on a cycle*" (subject to giving way to pedestrians & persons on horse, CA 68 s30; Countryside Act 1968 s.30);

c) byway open to all traffic (BOAT):- *"a highway over which the public has a right of way for vehicular (horse-drawn or motorised) and other kinds of traffic, but which is used mainly for walking, for horseriding or cycling"*.

d) road used as a public path (RUPP):-is a category due to be reclassified as either a footpath, a bridleway or a byway but meanwhile has at least bridleway status (WCA 81 s 54; Wildlife & Countryside Act 1981). They are currently recorded on the Oxfordshire Definitive Map & Statement as:-

d(i) CRB :- "*carriage road used mainly as a bridleway*"; or

d(ii) CRF :- "*carriage road used mainly as a footpath*".

e) motorway:- *"road specially constructed for motor vehicles, with separate carriage-ways for two directions, without a level crossing with any other track, without access to bordering properties and prohibited to certain kinds of traffic, e.g. pedestrians, provisional drivers, riders of horses and cycles, slow moving vehicles etc.*" (UN Convention, Vienna, 1968).

other roads (trunk, A, B & C roads & unclassified county roads) are normally open to all traffic (except types specified in a local traffic regulation order).

carriageway:- *"a way (other than a cycle track) constituting or comprised in a highway and being a public right of way for vehicles*" (includes a right of way on foot, horseback and cycle)

cycle track:- "*a way constituting or comprised in a highway and being a public right of way for pedal cycles (with/without a right of way on foot)"*

footway:- "*a public right of way on foot only, comprised in a highway which also comprises a carriageway*".

The above terms refer either to an abstract idea (a right) or to a physical object (a road) or to both. Other terms, not legally defined (e.g. in HA 80), but in common parlance,:-

green lane "*an unsurfaced way, often between hedges*";

pavement:- (in Highway Code) syn. of "*footway*";

verge:- "*unsurfaced road area, not carriageway, cycle track nor footway"*

easement:- "*private right of way over property of adjoining landowners*" (it may additionally carry public rights of way.

permissive path:- "*path or track which a landowner permits the public to use as a concession, possibly subject to conditions"* (eg. periodic closure, annual payments, dogs to be on leads, etc.).

3. Ownership and liability.

Land for a motorway, a trunk or classified road is normally compulsorily acquired by the State whereas other public rights of way generally run over land in private ownership, e.g. a footpath or bridleway across a field.

The surface of a publicly maintained pathis vested in the highway authority (which is, therefore, liable for users who are injured e.g. because the surface is in disrepair from potholes, slippery stones, tree stumps), not in the land owner or occupier. On a "permissive" route, liability for the surface rests with the private landholder (Occupiers Liability Act 1957 s2).

Gates and stiles, ("field furniture"), are the property of the landowner who alone is able to give permission for way-marking them and who has a duty to maintain such structures "*in a safe condition and to the standard of repair required to prevent unreasonable interference with the rights of the persons using the footpath or bridleway*" (HA 80 s146). A contribution of "*not less than 25%"* of the cost is available from the O.C.C. either in cash or in kit form.

4. Responsibilities for maintenance & protection.

The Highway Authority is the Oxfordshire County Council (O.C.C.) which is responsible for the following specified duties (HA 80 s1):-

a) to maintain publicly maintainable highways (HA 80 s 41 & 42);

b) to keep a list of such highways for public inspection (HA 80 s 36);

c) to "assert and protect" the rights of the public in their safe use & enjoyment and to prevent obstruction of paths (HA 80 s130);

d) to enforce the restoration of footpaths & bridleways lawfully ploughed up and to take action where ploughing or other disturbance was unlawful (HA 80 s 134 & 131A);

e) to enforce the duty of an occupier to ensure that crops do not inconvenience users of footpaths, bridleways and unmetalled carriageways (HA 80 s137A);

f) to signpost & waymark footpaths, bridleways and byways (CA 68 s27, as amended by Wildlife & Countryside Act 1981 WCA81 s 64);

g) to prosecute anyone responsible for misleading notices on/near a public path (National Parks & Access to the Countryside Act '49, s57).

The surveying authority (also the O.C.C.) is statutarily responsible for:-

a) keeping the Definitive Map under continuous review; including making modification orders and making copies of the Definitive Map and Statement publicly available (WCA 81 s 53 & s 57);

b) reclassifying RUPPs (WCA 81 s 54).

The Parish Councils have no duties, but do have some powers which may contribute to the public enjoyment of rights of way.

The land owner or occupier is responsible for:-

a) keeping the path free from side growth or overhanging growth, including crops other than hay & silage (on bridleways, riders should be allowed 3 metres or 10 feet of headroom) and

b) keeping the path free from other obstructions (rubbish, barbed wire, electric fences etc.)

c) keeping gates & stiles safe and convenient for users.

5. Ordnance Survey (O.S.) maps.

The O.S. *Landranger* maps (1:50,000 scale) show towns, villages and major topographical features (woods, contours, motorways, A-roads and B-roads in different colours). They are most useful for initial route planning as they also mark public footpaths, bridleways and BOATS using information derived from county Definitive Maps.

The O.S. *Pathfinder* maps (1:25,000 scale) are more detailed and show field boundaries, parish boundaries and additional place names of farms etc. They are most useful for route following. They also distinguish clearly between cross-field and field-edge paths (see para.9 Q.3 below).

6. The "Definitive Map and Statement" (DMS).

The initial survey in 1950 of all public rights of way required county councils under the National Parks & Access to the Countryside Act 1949 (NPACA 49) to produce a draft map. Properly carried out, it entailed an immense amount of work and progress was protracted because of lack of resources, although Oxfordshire produced a first draft review by January 1968 (North Bedfordshire was completed only in 1982).

The number of public paths in North Oxfordshire alone is considerable:-

	Total paths, of which	Bridleways	BOATS/RUPPS
Cherwell	1,153	234	35
West Oxon.	1,200	260	50

But these numbers are misleading since rights of way were recorded within parishes and one continuous path on the ground will be recorded separately in each of the parishes it traverses. A path may be recorded with a different status in an adjoining parish or county (eg. changing at the border from a BOAT to a bridleway or footpath), so that it is effectively a continuous right of way on foot only. Some Oxfordshire paths are, by administrative orders, cul-de-sacs which terminate at the M40; others have become virtual cul-de-sacs by traffic density on roads like the A34 or A420. Several rights of way are quite unusable.
The DMS provides in all cases conclusive evidence only of what is shown, so that what is shown as a footpath may nevertheless be of higher status under WCA 81 s56(1)(a) and *R v Devon CC, ex parte Fowler* (1990).

> "The DMS may be incomplete or inaccurate for several reasons so that they should be regarded merely as the starting point in determining what rights of way exist across an area of land". (p.16 *Managing Public Access, a guide for farmers & landowners"* by the CLA, NFU & Countryside Commission, 1994).

7. D.M.S. Modifications.

In Oxfordshire, there is a backlog of 3 years work in applications to modify the DMS, including 450 current "legal event" orders and a further 2,000 to be covered in future. Additionally a number of public paths are obstructed by walls, fences, farm buildings and even dining rooms.

> "1,300 current obstructions on public paths, including 55 where the definitive line is totally blocked" ("*Public Rights of Way, Milestone Statement*", O.C.C 1995).

The *Milestone Statement* suggested that some of the work might never be achieved without further resources.

8. The maps and text in this booklet.

OS Landranger (1:50,000) **maps** have been photocopied with the permission of the Controller of Her Majesty's Stationery Office, © Crown Copyright, conditional upon a scale enlargement/reduction of 20%.
The following **symbols** (see map of Oxfordshire) have been super-imposed:-
a) dashes (broken lines) for sections on bridlepaths and byways;
b) lines (unbroken lines) for sections on roads;
c) dots for other bridleways (to join, curtail or extend a route);
d) numbers for points on route and e) letters for alternative sections or routes.
O.S. Grid references (GR.) are Eastings (L. to R.), then Northings (upwards).
Font styles in the text indicate the route (ordinary font), place-names on OS Landranger maps (**bold**), and features of interest (*italics*).

9. Some questions and answers.

Q. 1. How wide is a public path?

A. 1. The DMS may indicate a width, for example, Bridleway No.1 in the parish of Sibford Ferris is specified to be "12 feet wide" in an Inclosure Award. Normally there is no width indicated in the DMS and there is no statutory minimum width for public paths, except after ploughing. Common sense dictates a minimum width but sufficient for two walkers, horse riders or cyclists and carriages to pass safely in opposite directions.

Q. 2. Is Ploughing allowed?

A.2(i). NO, in respect of "field edge" footpaths, bridleways & byways, these being defined as "*paths which follow the sides or headlands of a field or enclosure*" (HA 80 s.329).

A.2(ii). YES, in respect of cross-field footpaths & bridleways, (including other disturbance incidental to agricultural cropping), but subject to two duties:-

a) making good the surface within 14 days (weather permitting),

b) indicating the line of the path across the field.

Q. 3. What is the minimum width of path? (to be made good, to be indicated or to be left undisturbed ?) (RoWA 1990 s.1):-

A.3.

	footpath	bridleway	BOAT
cross-field	1.0 metres	2 metres	3 metres
field edge	1.5 metres	3 metres	5 metres

These widths must be usable minimum widths, i.e. excluding ditches, fences, hedges etc. Many farmers use a tractor to leave "tramlines" indicating the path line after disturbance and before the crop has grown sufficiently to allow crop spraying or cutting (2 metres is the overall wheel width of a medium size tractor).

Q. 4. Is barbed wire permitted? (i.e."*wire with jagged projections or spikes")*

A.4(i). Barbed wire placed alongside a narrow path where it can be dangerous or injurious to persons/clothing and/or to horses must be removed (HA 80 s164).

A.4(ii). Where it is put across the path, it is an "obstruction" and a crime by statute (HA 80 s137).

Q. 5. The erection of gates & stiles. A right of way may be dedicated subject to the right of the owner to place gates, stiles or barriers across it and such limitations should be recorded in the DMS. Otherwise authorisation is required and is given for certain agricultural or forestry operations (HA 80 s147).

Q. 6. What about bridges? (to replace a ford or stepping stones) The O.C.C. has the power but no obligation to improve a highway surface(HA 80 s91).

Q. 7. Should gates be left shut?, open? or "as found"?

A.7. Occasionally the occupier requires them left open to permit repeated passage of machinery between arable fields (e.g. silage- or grain-carrying trailers) or of livestock between pasture fields (for watering or milking purposes). The BHS recommends they be "left as found". The CLA recently recommended, to avoid all ambiguity, that gates be shut unless they are clearly tied back, open, by the occupier.

Q. 8. Are bulls, dogs & stallions allowed?

Bulls are prohibited in fields crossed by a right of way (WCA 81 s59) except:-

a) young bulls (up to 10 months), and

b) bulls not of a "recognised dairy breed" when running with cows or heifers (viz. not Ayrshire, British Friesian, British Holstein, Dairy Shorthorn, Guernsey, Jersey, Kerry").

Dogs, on a lead or under close control, are allowed on a public right of way.

Stallions, or other animals having "*characteristics likely to cause severe damage*" or injury make their keepers liable (The Animals Act 1971 s2 or the Health & Safety at Work Act 1974 s3)

Riders have a responsibility to move slowly through or past all stock at pasture to avoid panic among sheep, cattle, outdoor pigs & horses, especially when they may be in-lamb, in-calf etc.

Q. 9. How to deal with obstructions and nuisances ?

A.9(i). The first step is to report to the occupier (if known) who may be unaware of a fallen tree, a landslide, broken gate etc. and who can advise on an acceptable diversion. Sometimes bad weather may legitimately delay his remedial work.

A.9(ii). The second step is to report to the O.C.C., which has a duty to remove obstructions and to abate nuisances (HA 80 s130), especially where these appear to be man-made (a locked gate, electric fencing or barbed wire). A copy of O.C.C. "*Rights of way report form*" is published in this booklet.

A.9(iii). A private individual cannot bring an action unless he has himself suffered injury or loss but under common law he is legally entitled to abate it himself by:-

a) removing so much of the obstruction as is necessary to continue his journey conveniently and safely (*Seaton v. Slama* 1932) and to carry for this purpose a small pair of secateurs or wire cutters; and

b) deviating around obstacles (e.g. boggy ground) found on a public right of way which might endanger life or limb of ramblers, riders or horses. Because a user cannot be certain who holds the adjoining land, care should be taken to avoid damage during inadvertent trespass on any adjoining land.

10. Road safety ("BE SEEN - - BE SAFE").

Riding clothes should be safe, secure and light coloured.

Flourescent/reflective materials are more visible to drivers of motor vehicles under dipped headlights at night or in wet weather (e.g a body tabard, a "Sam Browne" shoulder belt or velcro strips around cannon bones / brushing boots).

"The Highway Code", HMSO, New Edition 1993, has nine excellent rules for horse riders, including two legal obligations (Rules 218 & 222):-

a) Riders under 14 MUST wear approved safety helmets securely fastened
b) Horses MUST NOT be taken on a footpath, pavement or cycle track.

No road is absolutely safe since speeding motorists, often late and talking on a mobile phone, can be found on any minor rural road throughout Oxfordshire. Many horseriders are car drivers, some are lorry drivers, and consequently are well aware of the problems of motoring behind or close to horse riders and carriage drivers. Most motorists are not.

The horse rider has three advantages over the motorist:-

a) he has wider experience,
b) he can better hear vehicles, even from two directions,
c) he can see over hedges and round bends, better and before a motorist overtaking from behind. He can, therefore, judge earlier whether and when it is unsafe to be overtaken.

A rider's signals should be early, clear and unambiguously informative before the manoeuvre, then courteous afterwards. Such signals, in my experience, are appreciated and acknowledged politely by Oxfordshire car and lorry drivers almost without exception.

Riding in groups in pairs at most (changing to "in strings" along narrow roads)

a) more experienced horses/riders go outside (and at the front / tail),
b) 100 ft. is best kept between groups (& 4 ft between horses, nose to tail),
c) defensive riding deters motorists overtaking on blind bends/ narrow bridges
d) one leader / tailer decides the changes and ensures group communication.

11. Route Riding.

Daily physical exercise on local roads and public paths is a normal routine of 60 to 90 minutes duration for horses in many disciplines (flatracing, hurdling, chasing, P-to-P., team events, dressage, hunting, show jumping and endurance riding). Route riding is different and the extra work of "boxing up" to do a distant route has to be balanced against the benefit of mental fitness coming from a change of scenery.

Circular routes can take three to five hours, depending on numbers of gates, weather conditions etc. Winter brings short days, overcast or foggy conditions and icy or boggy ground. Journeys are slower and need a greater allowance for contingencies such as detours or lost shoes. Summer can bake boggy clay paths into concrete-like surfaces with potholes. This is also the season of splints, flies & sunburn. The horse, a browsing animal, needs periodically a chance to graze and water (cavalry had routine stops to rest and to "bait").

A new route, in any case, takes more time: time to read a map and compass, time to talk to strangers, time to go slowly past possible hazards (farm stock, rabbit holes or fallen trees and fencing wire).

Valediction.

Henry Peacham, (whose "*Compleat Gentleman*" in 1622 established a tradition of "courtesy" books describing the proper education of a member of the court some 30 years before Izaak Walton's "*The Compleat Angler*"), recommended riding as good for body and mind:-

> "*...the most pleasing of all is riding with a good horse and a good companion, in the spring or summer season, into the country when the blossoms are on the trees and flowers in the fields, or when corn and fruit are ripe in autumn. ....low meadows, ..crystal streams, woody hills, parks with deer, ...churches, villages, the houses of gentlemen and husbandmen, ...variety of country labours and exercises..and if you happen to converse with countrymen of the place, you will find them, for the most part, understanding enough...*"

The author has had that pleasure and privilege for the last three years, as an O.A.P. on a retired racehorse with various riding companions (not forgetting a Jack Russell). He can only hope that this booklet enables and encourages others to have the same experience and pride in the Oxfordshire countryside.[1]

OXFORDSHIRE COUNTY COUNCIL *RIGHTS OF WAY REPORT FORM*

Please complete this form, as fully as possible, and return it to:
The Department of Leisure and Arts,
Countryside Service, Library HQ, HOLTON, Oxford, OX9 1QQ.

<table>
<tr><td colspan="2">Parish:</td><td colspan="2">Type of route and definitive map number:
Footpath
Bridleway
Byway, etc</td></tr>
<tr><td colspan="4">Name and address of Landowner/Occupier:</td></tr>
<tr><td>Ordnance Survey
Grid Reference(s):</td><td colspan="3">Details of problem(s) including date noted:
Continue overleaf if necessary.</td></tr>
<tr><td colspan="3">Your name, address and telephone number:</td><td>Name of Organisation:

Date:</td></tr>
<tr><td colspan="4">Action taken (for office use):

Clearing House Reference:</td></tr>
</table>

EQUINE & EQUESTRIAN BED & BREAKFAST

Bed & Breakfast is normally provided for both horse & rider, but some addresses may provide B&B for one and arrange B&B for the other nearby.

Mr. Dudley Osbourne, Weston Manor Hotel, Weston on the Green, Bicester
Oxon OX6 8QL (tel.01869.350621)
Mrs. Lorna Godwin, Manor Farm, Oxford Road, Weston on the Green,
Bicester, Oxon OX6 8QL (tel.01869.350354)
Mrs. Julie Strachey, Southfield Farm, North Lane, Weston-on-the Green,
Bicester, Oxon OX6 8RG (tel.01869 350833)
Mrs. Carolyne Henman, Mill Farm, Mill Lane, Islip, Oxon. OX (tel.01865 375454)
Mr. Andrew Green, Greenhill Farm, Bletchingdon Oxford, OX5 3BQ-
(mobile 0374.740514 (tel.01869.350271)
Mrs. Judith Hunter, Vicarage Farm, Kirtlington, Oxford, OX5 3Y- (tel.01869.650254)
Mrs Sue Eeley, Northbrook Farm, Kirtlington Oxon. OX5 3HY (tel.01869 350258)
Toddy & Clive Hamilton-Gould, Tower Fields, Tusmore Rd., Souldern,
near Bicester, Oxon. OX6 9HY (tel.01869 345157)
Mrs Joan White, Hill Barn, Milton Gated Road, Deddington, Banbury,
Oxon. OX15 OTS (tel.01869.338631)
Mr. John Kelly, South Lodge Riding School, Caversfield, Bicester, Oxon (tel.01869.243934)
Mrs. D. Pritchard, Edgehill Farmhouse, Edge Hill, Nr. Banbury, Oxon. OX15 6HS
(tel.01295 670383)
Mrs. Juliet McKenzie, Ivy Cottage, Culworth ,Banbury, Oxon, OX17 2AP (tel.01295 768131)
Mrs. Ros Thompstone, Lockhill Farm, Ratley, Banbury,Oxon. OX15 6DS. (tel.01295 670272)
Mrs. Rosemary Nunneley, Sugarswell Farm, Shennington, Banbury,
OX15 6HW. (tel.01295 688188 / 01295 680512)
Mrs. Vicki Patrick, The Manor House, The Green, Hornton, Near Banbury,
OX15 6BZ (tel.01295 670386)
Mrs. Jane Lee, The Mill Barn, Lower Tadmarton, Nr. Banbury, Oxon.
OX15 5SU (tel.01295 780349)
Mr. & Mrs. Roger Nicholls, "*Horse & Groom*" PH, Milcombe, Nr. Banbury, Oxon.
(tel.01295 720471)
Mrs. Grete Ricketts, Banner Hill Farm, Quainton, Bucks HP22 4AQ (tel.01296.75543)
Mrs. Collett, Manor Farm, Poundon, Bucks (tel.01869.277212)
Mrs. Thornton, Blackheath Farm Stables, Milton-U-Wychwood, Nr. Burford
Oxon. OX7 6HX (tel.01993.823365)
Mrs. Sarah Potter, Lees Rest Farm, Charlbury, Oxon. OX7 3EU, (tel.01608 810388)
Mark & Arvinda Finniear, Oldner Stables, Charlbury Road, Chipping Norton,
Oxon. OX7 5XH (tel.01608 643914)
Mrs P.Hunt, North Farm, Fairley Lane, Stonesfield, Nr. Charlbury (tel.01993 891231)
Mr. & Mrs. David Parris, Stone Farm, Lidstone, nr Enstone, Oxon. (tel.01608 677088)
Mrs. Jenny Badger, UK Chasers No.26, Crown Farm, Ascott-u-Wychwood,
Oxon. OX7 6AB (tel.01993.830307)
Jane Hankey, John Beswick, Pebbly Hill Stud, Bledington, Glos. (tel.01608.659743)
"*The Merrymouth*" PH, Stow Rd, Fifield, Near Burford, Oxon...... (tel.01993.831652)
Mrs. Pam Gee, Denmans Farm, Farmoor, Oxford, Oxon. OX2 9NJ (tel.01865 862386)
Mr. David Gow, West Farm, Eaton, Abingdon, Oxon. OX13 5PR (tel.01865 864607)
Mrs. Pat Blanchard, Newhouse Farm Stables & Livery, Southmoor,
Nr Abingdon OX13 (tel.01865 821180)
Mrs. Hazel Smith, Delphinium Cottage, Oxford Rd Grove, Wantage,
Oxon. OX12 7PE (tel.01235 763649)

B&B (ctd)
Mrs. Penny Reid, Down Barn Farm, Sparsholt Down, Wantage, Oxon. OX12 9XD (tel.01367 820272)
Mrs. Wendy Grant, Monks Farm Stables, Newbury Rd, East Hendred, Nr.Wantage, Oxon OX12 8LG (tel.01235 820107)
Mrs. Viv Haigh, Orpwood House, School Rd., Ardington, Wantage, Oxon OX12 8PN (tel.01235 833300)
Mr. & Mrs. K.A. Rugge-Price, Stainswick Manor, Bourton, Shrivenham, Wilts. SN.8LD (mobile 0850 916604 (tel.01793.784133)
Mrs. J Callam-Anderson, Lyntbridge Farmhouse, Inglesham, Nr Lechlade, Wilts. SN6.7RE (tel.01367.252006)
Pat & Geof Mason, "*The Lamb*" PH., Filkins Near Lechlade, Glos. (tel.01367.860300)
Mrs. Pat Hoddinott, Ashen Copse Farm, Coleshill, Highworth, Swindon, Wilts. SN6 7PU (tel.01367 240175)
Mrs. Vickie Mace, Wickstead Fm Equestrian Centre, Highworth, Swindon, Wilts. SN6 7PP (tel.01793 762265)
"The White Horse" PH, Woolstone, Uffington, Nr.Faringdon (tel.01367 820726)
Mrs. Sylvia Cox, Sower Hill Farm, Woolstone, SN7 7QH (tel.01367 820758)
Mrs. D. Barnards, Bowling Green Farm, Stanford Road, Faringdon, Oxon. SN7 8EZ (tel.01367 240229)
"*The Horse & Jockey*" PH., Downs Road, Chilton, nr Harwell (tel.01235.820811)
Mrs. Jacky Taylor, Chilton, near Harwell. (tel.01235.831942)
Sandra Saunders, Ridgeway Farm Livery, Chilton, near Harwell. (tel.01235.821137)
Lady Shuckburgh, High Wood House, Greenfield Watlington, OX9 5HG (tel.01491 612433)
Mrs. D.T.Belcher, Hale Farm, Benson, OX10 6NE (tel.01491 836818)
Mrs. Sue Clayton, Lower Farm, Berrick Salome, Benson, Oxon., OX9 6JL (tel 01865.891073)
Lady Bridget Silsoe, Neals Farm, Wyfold, Checkenden, Reading Berks (tel.01491 680258)
Mr.& Mrs. H. Brooks, Jackson's Farm, Fawley Bottom, Henley-on-Thames, Oxon RG9 6JJ (tel.01491 575330)

35 A Country Inn
From an engraving of 1791

EQUINE VETERINARY PRACTICES

A list for emergency purposes published by courtesy of the Royal College of Veterinary Surgeons.

Cherwell	
J. Digby Hodgins, Weston on the Green, Bicester	tel:-01869 343567
Ferens, Cummings & Cornish, Bicester.	tel:-01869 252077
The Hart Veterinary Centre, Bicester.	tel:-01869 323223
Walker & Glanvill, Hook Norton	tel:-01608 730085
Avonvale Veterinary Group, Ratley, Banbury	tel:-01295 670501
Hawthorn Lodge Veterinary Surgery, Banbury	tel:-01295 59446
West Bar Veterinary Hospital, Banbury & Adderbury	tel:-01295 267531
West Oxfordshire	
Aylmer & Cannon, Chipping Norton	tel:-01608 642547
Parkwood Veterinary Group, Woodstock & Eynsham	tel:-01993 811355
Jackson Veterinary Clinic, Carterton & Witney	tel:-01993 842717
Walker & Glanvill, Charlbury	tel:-01608 730085
A.C. Pickles, Fulbrook, Burford	tel:-01993 823670
Vale of White Horse (incl.Oxford)	
Larkmead Veterinary Group, Abingdon & Didcot	tel:-01491 651479
Parkwood Veterinary Group, Didcot & Kidlington	tel:-01993 811355
Danetree Veterinary Surgeons, Faringdon	tel:-01367 242777
Alternative Vet. Medicine Centre, Stanford in the Vale	tel:-01367 710324
Beaumont Veterinary Hospital, Oxford & Kidlington	tel:-01865 243225
A. Bartholomew Oxford & Wheatley	tel:-01865 242600
South Oxon	
Larkmead Veterinary Group, Benson & Cholsey	tel:-01491 651479
Barbara Bennett, Tiddington, Thame	tel:-01844 279999
Dovecourt Veterinary Group, Wallingford	tel:-01491 839043
N.E. de Baan & Associates, Henley on Thames	tel:-01491 574490
Gibbons & Sprinz, Thame & Chinor	tel:-01844 212000

43 A Postchaise, leaving Oxford, halted at the Turnpike on the London Road

From a drawing of ca. 1800

FARRIERS

This Oxfordshire County list is published by courtesy of The Farriers Registration Council and is printed under licence from the copyright information in the Council's Register dated 19/01/96.

Part I

Andrews, David Michael 14/06/80 DWCF 24/04/80-043 Tel:-01608 683280
Meetings Farm, Little Tew, Enstone, Oxon OX7 4JN

Belcher, Ian 01/04/82 DWCF 12/03/82-127 Tel:-01235 850029
6 Bridus Mead, Blewbury, Didcot Oxon OX11 9PJ

Belcher, Michael Edward 21/08/76 BII 01/01/56 Tel:-01235 850571
34 Eastfields, Blewbury, Didcot Oxon OX11 9NS

Cherry, Roland John 01/01/78 RSS 30/06/72-10390 Tel:-01608 658552
Forge Side, Hastings Hill, Churchill, Oxon OX7 6NA

Cox, John Henry 01/01/86 RSS 15/04/53-9873 Tel:-01869 253624
79 Murcott Road, Arncott, Bicester, Oxon OX6 OPL

Davison, Andrew Peter 01/10/82 DWCF 12/03/82-134 Tel:-01
Garden Cottage, Woolley, Nr Wantage, Oxon OX12 8NJ

Dewdney,Derek Barrie 01/01/83 RSS 02/06/65-10129 Tel:-01491 572155
107 Harpsden Road, Henley on Thames, Oxon RG9 1ED

Feltham, Giles Peter 01/09/91 DWCF 05/03/91-608 Tel:-01235 760165
6 Upthorpe Drive, Wantage Oxon OX12 7DF

Godfrey, Tom David 01/11/94 DWCF 26/08/94-/786 Tel:-01235 868492
Brook Cottage Farm, Charney Basset, Wantage, Oxon OX12 OEN

Gulley, Michael 01/07/84 AWCF 17/10/90-848 DWCF Hons 15/03/84-268 Tel:-01295 730135
Ivydene, Church St, Ascott u Wychwood, Oxon OX7 6AZ

Hall, Alfred 09/10/85 DWCF 09/10/85-357 Tel:-01367 710566
Station House, Challow Station, Faringdon, Oxon SN7 8NT

Harman, Daniel Edward 01/11/94 DWCF 25/08/94-/789 Tel:-01844 216780
86A Coombe Hill Crescent, Thame Oxon OX9 2EH

Hicks, Andrew George 01/08/81 DWCF 26/06/61-088 Tel:-01608 642795
33 Rock Hill, Chipping Norton, Oxon OX7 5BA

Hiley, Roger 22/03/93 DWCF BII 26/05/95-847 Tel:-01869 242672
71 Shannon Road, Bicester Oxon OX6 8RN

Hows, Jonathan Victor 01/01/78 AFCL BI 14/06/76-729 RSS BII 03/06/74-10483
57 Ardington, Wantage, Oxon OX12 8PY Tel:-01865 833676

Johnson, Mark Eric John 09/07/83 DWCF 16/03/83-205 Tel:-01295 712276
16 Lexton Gardens, Middleton Cheney Banbury, Oxon OX17 2LA

Reed, Martin Christopher 01/01/87 DWCF 05/03/86-386 Tel:-01295............
2 St. George's Crescent, Banbury, Oxon OX16 9HN

Rowling, Martin Stephen 01/01/79 RSS 28/01/69-10261 Tel:-01295 76439
Culworth Forge Culworth, Banbury, Oxon

Smith, David Paul 01/10/84 AWCF 18/10/88-826 DWCF 15/03/84-281 Tel:-01608 642584
Little Meadows, Choice Hill, Over Norton, Oxon OX7 5PZ

Smith, William 01/01/81 FWCF 12/09/68-140 AFCL 04/12/62-583 RSS 24/09/54-9933
23 Watcombe Road, Watlington, Oxon OX9 5QJ Tel:-01491 612872

Thomas, Gary Haydn 01/10/84 DWCF 15/03/84-286 Tel:-01..................
2 Queens Cottages, West Street, Sparsholt, Wantage Oxon

Watkins, Michael George. 01/01/78 RSS 31/08/62-10050 Tel:-01608 642897
7 Rock Hill, Chipping Norton, Oxon OX7 5BA

Webb, Trevor Mark 01/04/86 DWCF 09/10/85-360 Tel:-01235 765307
50 Blenheim Gardens, Grove, Wantage, Oxon OX12 ONP

Wilson, Paul Sliegh 01/04/87 DWCF 07/10/86-436 Tel:-01865 376890
14 Jerome Way, Shipton on Cherwell, Oxon OX5 1JT

Part II

Cooper, David Charles 25/05/77 Tel:-01367 810317
Edgerley Farm, Clanfield, Nr. Bampton, Oxon OX18 2SB

Denziloe-Killick, David 01/01/83 Tel:-01993 775555
6 Cotswold Close, Minster Lovell, Oxon OX8 5SX

Gascoigne, Ronald Frank 01/01/79 Tel:-01869 340376
17 Worton Road, Middle Barton, Chipping Norton, Oxon OX7 7EE

Holmes, Graham Lionel 01/01/80 Tel:-01869 350641
Star House, Charlton on Otmoor, Kidlington, Oxon OX5 2TZ

McCulloch, Ian Walker 01/11/81 Tel:-01
19 Western Avenue, Henley on Thames, Oxon RG9 1JP

McOwen, Michael 01/02/78 Tel:-01
Flat 3 Montpelier House, High Street, Harwell, Nr. Didcot, Oxon OX11 OER

Morgan, Albert Richard 01/01/78 Tel:-01295 730601
The Forge, North Newington, Banbury Oxon

Onions, John 01/01/79 Tel:-01993 830128
Pilgrim Cottage, High Street, Milton u Wychwood, Oxon

Richings, Mervyn Victor 26/05/77 Tel:-01367 820253
Wharf Bungalow, Uffington, Faringdon, Oxon SN7 7PS

Strong, Anthony Roy 01/01/79 Tel:-01865 59326
13 Meadow Prospect, Wolvercote, Oxford OX2 8PP

Timms, Robert Graham 01/01/78 Tel:-01844 214853
76 Aylesbury Road, Thame, Oxon OX9 3AY

Part IV

Harbour, Ian Frank 14/04/92 Tel:-01844 352365
8 Hunters Point, Chinor, Oxon. OX9 4TG

New, David 01/01/83 Tel:-01..................
Appleyree Cottage, Mallins Lane, Longcot, Faringdon, Oxon.

NB.

FWCF Fellow of the Worshipful Company of Farriers

AWCF (or AFCL) Associate of the Worshipful Company of Farriers (formerly Associate of the Farriers Company of London)

DWCF (or RSS) Diploma of the Worshipful Company of Farriers (formerly Registered Shoeing Smith)

26 Shoeing a Horse, 1699

RIDING SCHOOLS & LIVERY STABLES

South Lodge, Caversfield, Bicester	tel:-01869 243934
Heathfield Equestrian Centre, Heathfield, Bletchington	tel:-01869 350227
Village Farm, Weston Road, Bletchington	tel:-01869 350257
Roy Kinch, Manor Farm, Steeple Aston	tel:-01869 340312
Hazel Offord, Wendlebury Gate Stables, Bicester	tel:-01869 252224
The Priory Stables, Chetwode, Bucks	tel:-01869 277082
Millbrook Arabian Stud & Livery Yard, Deddington	tel:-01869 338656
Valley Farm Equestrian Centre, Shotteswell, Nr. Banbury	tel:-01295 730576
Equisport Liveries, Barford St. John, Deddington	tel:-01295 721849
Manor Farm Livery, Wiggington, Banbury	tel:-01608 737246
Turpins Lodge Riding Centre, Lodge Fm., Hook Norton	tel:-01608 737033
Diana Green Liveries, High Martin Fm., Lower Tadmarton, Nr. Banbury	tel:-01295 780444
Finmere Equestrian Centre, Town Farm, Finmere	tel:-01280 847891
Kirtlington Park Polo School, Park Farm, Kirtlington	tel:-01869 350083
Oaklands Riding School, Upper Tysoe	tel:-01295 688045
Farnborough Livery Yard, nr. Banbury	tel:-01295 690504
Stonecroft Equestrian Centre, Oxhill, Warks, Nr. Banbury	tel:-01296 640373
Stowe Ridings Equestrian Centre, Stowe, Bucks	tel:-01280 812363
Furlong Riding School, Nether Westcote, Shipton u Wychwood	tel:-01993 831193
Jane Hankey, John Beswick, Pebbly Hill Stud, Bledington, Glos	tel:-01608.659743
Hailey Equitatian Centre, Poffley End, Witney	tel:-01993 702844
Yew Tree Stables, Abingdon Rd., Standlake	tel:-01865 300082
Thrupp Stables, Manor Fm., Kidlington	tel:-01865 842439
Worton Rectory Fm. Stables, Cassington	tel:-01865 883598
Cotswolds Traing Centre, Carterton	tel:-01993 842262
Odell W.J., Little Tew, Great Tew	tel:-01608.683249
Old Manor House Riding Sch., North Hinksey Lane, Oxford	tel:-01865 242274
Waterstock House Training Centre, Waterstock, Oxford	tel:-01865 339616
Oxford Riding School, Watlington Rd., Garsington	tel:-01865 361383
New House Livery, New House Fm, Hanney Rd., Southmoor	tel:-01865 821180
Oakfield Riding School, Great Coxwell, Faringdon	tel:-01367 240126
Wadley Manor Stables, Faringdon	tel:-01367 244413
The Asti Stud, Millaway Fm, Goosey, Faringdon	tel:-01367 710288
Gramps Hill Stud, Letcombe Bassett, Wantage	tel:-01235 73536
Malt House Equestrian Centre, Hanney Rd., Steventon	tel:-01235 831488
Silverdown Riding School, Reading Rd., Harwell, Didcot	tel:-01235 835377
Blewbury Riding & Training Centre, Blewbury, Didcot	tel:-01235 851016
Stonehill Riding School, Oday Hill, Drayton, Abingdon	tel:-01235 529915
Aston Equestrian Centre, Aston Rowant, Nr. Chinor	tel:-01844 352824
Blenheim Riding Centre, Benson, Nr. Wallingford	tel:-01491 836057
Mannanan Stables, Rosehill, Henley on Thames	tel:-01628 824078
Turville Valley Stud, Turville, Henley on Thames	tel:-01491 638338

THE CITY MAGNATE.

NOT TO BE TRUSTED.

LORD, FARMER, AND COCKNEY.

SADDLERS & other SUPPLIERS (equine & equestrian)

Peter Ray, Field & Farm Saddlers, Newton Morrell Fm., Finmere	tel:-01280 848048
The Tack Shop, 47F Broad Street Banbury	tel:-01295 269505
Anne Bloor, saddler, Williamscott Rd, Cropredy	tel:-01295 758297
Seeney's, Doltons Grain Silo, Kidlington	tel:-01865 59750
Fringford Feeds, Hall Fm., Fringford, Bicester	tel:-01869 277301
O.Shepherd & Son, Brackley, Northants	tel:-01280 702224
Midland Shire Farmers, Finmere, Bucks	tel:-01280 848551
Tingewick Feed Supplies, Murcott	tel:-01296 770110
Bodicote Flyover Farm Shop, Bodicote, Banbury	tel:-01295 270789
Crendon Saddlery, The Square, Long Crendon, Thame, Bucks	tel:-01844 208577
Peter Smith Saddlery, Shipton u Wychwood	tel:-01993 831306
Issy's Equestrian Supplies, Smith's Estate, Witney	tel:-01993 773782
Hawk Equestrian, Bridge Street, Witney	tel:-01993 778207
Witney Farm Supplies, Burford Rd., Witney	tel:-01993 704263
Westfield Saddlery, Westfield Fm, Churchill Rd., Chipping Norton	tel:-01608 642518
Midland Shire Farmers, Banbury Rd., Chipping Norton	tel:-01608 642071
Midland Shire Farmers, Stanton Harcourt Rd., Eynsham	tel:-01865 881556
Charlbury Saddlery, Charlbury	tel:-01608 811254
C.H.Brown & Son, 52/53 The Market, Oxford	tel:-01865 244700
Ken Langford, Eaton Rd., Appleton, Abingdon	tel:-01865 863774
Charles Hunt & Partners, Hithercroft Rd., Wallingford	tel:-01494 837207

37 A Stage-Wagon of *ca.* 1805

From an engraving by Pyne

MOUNTAIN BIKES & CYCLING SUPPLIERS

Banbury Cycles Ltd, 54 Bridge St., Banbury	tel:-01295 259349
Discount Bikes, 2 Bridge St., Banbury	tel:-01295 272757
Broadribbs, Sheep St., Bicester	tel:-01869 253170
Dentons Cycles, 294 Banbury Rd., Oxford	tel:-01865 53859
Dentons Cycles, 1 High St., Witney	tel:-01993 704979
Giles Cycles, 1 Alvescot Rd., Carterton	tel:-01993 842396
Bee-Line Bikes, 61-63 Cowley Rd., Oxford	tel:-01865 246615
Botley Rd. Cycles, 63 Botley Rd., Oxford	tel:-01865 723100
Behind Bars, Ock Street, Abingdon	tel:-01235 533287
Bragg Bicycles, 2 High St., Abingdon	tel:-01235 520034
Cycle King, 55 Walton St., Oxford	tel:-01865 516122
Castles, St. Mary's St., Wallingford	tel:-01491 836289
Thame Cycles, 69a Park St., Thame	tel:-01844 261520
Beans, Outdoor pursuits clothing & equipment, 86 Sheep St., Bicester	tel:-01869 346451

OTHER SPECIALISED SERVICES

Jocelyn Catering, Ivy Hatch, Cassington OX8 1DL	tel:-01865 882522
Central Horse News, Blenheim Cottage, Hornton OX15 6BS	tel:-01295 670639
David Beecroft, Plant hire & civil engineering contractor	tel:-01869 350394
Michael P.Field, Equine dentist, Barford St.Michael, OX5 4RF	tel:-01869 38820
Johnsons of Abingdon, Horsebox repairs & maintenance	tel:-01235 550832
Bicester Trailers, Troy, Somerton, Bicester	tel:-01869 345576
P.A.Turney Limited, Paddock mowers, Weston on the Green OX6 8TN	tel:-01869 343292
Ken Messer, Artist, 7 Severn Road, Chilton	tel:-01235 834361
J.E.Miller & B.Cartwright, Agricultural Engineers (mobile:-0973 636176)	tel:-01869 350577
John Stilgoe, Estate gardens & paddock rails, 30 Norris Road, Arncott	tel:-01869 252357
John Cavan, Landscape contractor, The Old Water Mill, Weston o Green	tel:-01869 350386
Axicon Group (Barcodes), Church Rd. Weston-o-the Green, Bicester OXU 8QP	tel:-01869 351166
U.K. Chasers Ltd., Otmoor Lane, Beckley, Oxford, OX3 9TD	tel:-01865 351688

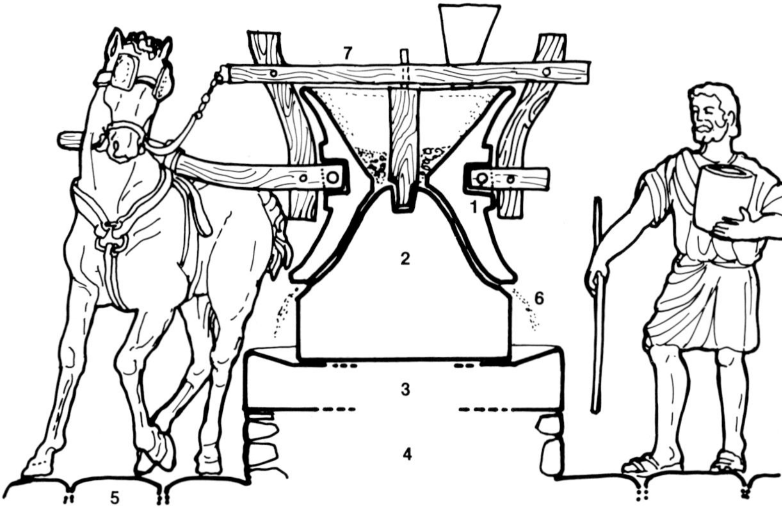

Section of a grindstone or donkey millstone and indication of how it worked
(from a relief in the Museo Nazionale Romano)

1 *Catillus*
2 *Meta*
3 Collecting basin
4 Base
5 Stone paved floor
6 Finest flour
7 Wooden Loom

ORGANIZATIONS

O.C.C Countryside Service, Dept. of Leisure & Arts, Holton, Oxon OX33 1QQ tel:-01865 810226
O.C.C Highways Engineer, Speedwell Ho., Speedwell St., Oxford tel:-01865 815700
B.C.C. Planning & Transportation Dept., County Hall, Aylesbury HP20 1UY tel:-01296 383205
Thames Valley Police HQ., Kidlington tel:-01865 846000
Banbury.........tel:-01295 252525 Bicester....................tel:-01869 320919
Witney...........tel:-01993 703913 Chipping Norton.......tel:-01608 642021
Wallingford....tel:-01235 512929 Faringdon/Wantage tel:-01235 776000
C.L.A. Regional Secretary, Brookfields Ho., Highclere, Newbury RG15 9RX tel:-01635 255412
N.F.U. Central region, Stanton Harcourt Rd., Eynsham, Witney, OX8 1 tel:-01865 882999
The Countryside Commission, Crescent Place, Cheltenham Glos. GL50 3RA - tel:-01242 521381
Council for the Protection of Rural England (CPRE), 25 Buckingham Palace Rd., London SW1W 0PP
British Driving Society, 27 Dugard Place, Barford nr. Warwick, CV35 8DX tel:-01926 624420
Riding for the Disabled Association, National Agric. Centre, Stoneleigh, Kenilworth tel:-01203 696595
The British Horse Society, Stoneleigh, Kenilworth, Warwickshire CV8 2LR tel:-01203 696697
Cyclists' Touring Club, 69 Meadrow, Godalming, Surrey GU7 3HS tel:-
The Ramblers Association, Hawkswell House & Gardens Oxford OX2 7EX tel:-
Long Distance Walkers Assoc., 9 Tainters Brook, Hempstead Fields, Uckfield East Sussex TN22 1UQ
Byways and Bridleways Trust, The Granary, Charlcutt, Calne, Wilts SN11 9HL
BBONT, 3 Church Cowley Rd., Rose Hill, Oxford OX4 3JR tel:-01865 775476
The Countryside Movement, Freepost, Bristol BS38 7HL tel:-01179 768900
The National Trust, Thames & Chilterns Regional Office, Hughenden Manor tel:-01494 528051
National Rivers Authority, Thames Region, Howbery Pk, Wallingford, OX4 4HJ tel:-01734 535000
Open Spaces Society, 25a Bell St., Henley on Thames, Oxon. RG9 2BA tel:-01491 573535
Oxford Fieldpaths Society, 21 Rowles Close, Kennington, Oxford, OX1 5LX tel:-01865 739092
The Royal Association for Disability & Rehabilitation, (RADA),
12 City Forum, 250 City Road, London ECIV 8AF tel:-0171 2503222
Sustrans, (Sustainable transport) (reg. Charity No.326550) 35 King Street, Bristol BS1 4DZ

FURTHER REFERENCE & READING

"OXFORDSHIRE", Joanna Cannan, Robert Hale Ltd. , 1975
"English Place-Names", A.D.Mills, O.U.P., 1993
"Bicester & Otmoor in Old Photographs", Sian Ellis, 1992
"National Trust Centenary Handbook for members & visitors", 1995
"The New Oxfordshire Village Book", Oxfordshire Federation of Women's Institutes, 1990
Roman Roads in Britain, South of the Foss Way-Bristol Channel, Ivan D. Margary, Phoenix Ho. Ltd., 1953
Circular Rides pack and Circular Walks pack, O.C.C.
"Oxfordshire Cycleway" Off-road cycling routes pack, O.C.C.
"The Oxfordshire Way - A walker's guide", O.C.C., 1993
"Oxfordshire Country Walks: No. 1 Evenlode & Wychwood", O.C.C., 1990
"Oxfordshire Country Walks: No.2 Chilterns" 1990, O.C.C.
"Oxfordshire Country Walks: No.3 Otmoor" 1992, O.C.C.
"Oxfordshire Country Walks: No.4 Upper Thames & Vale" , O.C.C.
Programme of Events, Winter & Summer, Cherwell District Council
Highways Act 1980, Chapter 66,(amended) London HMSO
Rights of Way Act 1990, Chapter 24, London HMSO
"Rights of Way, a guide to law and practice", John Riddell & John Trevelyan, 2nd edition, 1992
"Managing Public Access, a guide for farmers & landowners" CLA, NFU & the Countryside Commission.
"Out in the Country", Countryside Commission, 1992.
The Highway code, new edition 1993 HMSO.

69 Omnibuses in the Strand, *ca.* 1850

18 miles, circular, (anti-clockwise)
Ordnance Survey maps:
Landranger 164,
Pathfinder 1069, 1068, 1092
Length:
18 miles (29 km) in total, of which
12 miles (19 km) bridleway.
Several shorter alternatives.

Parking & starting points
a) "*Sturdy's Castle*" PH (GR.462193) on the A4260, Oxford & Kidlington to Banbury road. Large carpark but please phone 01869 83200 or 83328.
b) verge, Church Lane, Steeple Barton.

Route description

Start. From "*Sturdy's Castle*", take the "green lane" bridleway which immediately adjoins the PH and go west towards **Wootton.** Shortly after leaving "Sturdy's Castle" you cross a footpath *(which is Akeman Street, the Roman road running from Cirencester to Bicester).*

1. After 1 km, where a bridleway joins on the left from Woodstock, turn right and ride due north on a "green lane" past **Upper Dornford Fm.** cottages.

2. Cross a minor road at **Rousham Gap** (GR.460255)(3 km). Continue north on a farm track which goes through the yard of **Newbarn Fm.** and passes **Barton Lodge** on your right. Enter the farm gate into **Steeple Barton Abbey Park** (2 km)

3. Leave the Abbey Park (GR.453253) and turn right onto a minor road for 200 m to the "T" road-junction on the B4030. Cross to the good verge opposite (CARE) and turn left towards **Enstone** for 250 m. At the bend (CARE) take the field bridleway on the right, via two cattle-grid gates in succession, into **Whistlow Farm** yard (GR.452256). Continue north to the end of the third field, where a bridleway from **Brasenose Fm.** joins from the right. Turn west along a righthand hedge for two fields to a minor road (Middle Barton to Duns Tew).

4. Go north along the road (verge) for one field and then take a farm track bridleway on your left down to **Cockley Brook** (GR.452267). Cross the brook onto a field-edge bridleway on rising ground. Continue northwest on a cross-field bridleway over one field, over a bridleway at right angles (from Duns Tew to Middle Barton) and across a second field to join a bridleway coming from Duns Tew. Turn left westwards along the field edge track for one field

5. Turn right just north of **Down Hill Fm.** (GR.435271) for 300 m along a minor road (from Middle Barton to Over Worton). After Heath Cottage Farm, take the field-edge bridleway on your left (GR435275) along the south side of **Worton Wood** to its western corner. Ride northwest diagonally across an "L" shaped field to its inner corner. Turn west for two more fields and enter a lane into **Ledwell** (*O.E.word meaning " loud spring or well*")

6. Bear left to the cross roads and take the road opposite towards Great Tew & Little Tew. After 500 m turn right, down a farmtrack bridleway going north. Keep **Hobbshole Farm** on your right (GR.411291) and immediately below the farm buildings find a bridleway track which contours left, westwards. The field-edge bridleway leads across three fields and beside a walled park and

woodland to a gated path, at the back of the "*Falkland Arms*" PH. on the village green at **Great Tew**. *This village of thatched, Cotswold stone cottages possibly derives its name from O.E 'tiewe' meaning "row or ridge".*

7. Turn right, then left on the road above the school and ride past the Church to rejoin the Little Tew road to Ledwell. Bear left and take the first road on the right (signed "To Beaconsfield & Tracey Fms. only") (GR.401287). Go due south for 1.7 km where the road becomes a bridleway track. Ford the River Dorn at Poor Bridge and on rising ground go south then southeast past a WW II airfield, now private, onto a concrete track leading into a spinney. Turn left to **Cuckold's Holt Fm.** (GR.410256).

8. Join the B4030 and go east for 100 m (verge) to the "T" road-junction signposted **Sandford St. Martin**. Cross the B4030 (CARE) into the field bridleway opposite via double fieldgates. Turn southeast along a left-hand hedge (one field), then along a right-hand hedge (two fields) into a spinney between **Oathill Farm** on your right and Benneton Formula I **Wks.** on your left. Go left along the farm road (or the field-edge bridleway in the field opposite) to the minor road (Sandford St. Martin to Wootton).

9. Turn right, going south, along this road for 4 km, with 3 km of good verges, passing **White House Farm** and **Home Farm** (GR.429220). Then join and bear left along the B4027 (CARE - no verge) to the "*Killingworth Castle*" PH at **Wootton** (GR.433203).

10. Continue along the B4027 (verge) up to the cross-roads (a minor road from Wootton to Rousham Gap). Ride down (initially with a verge) to Milford Bridge over the River Dorn (GR.446198). After 200 m of sharply rising road (CARE), turn left onto the farm track leading to **Lower Dornford Farm** (GR.448199) After 300 m, and before the first house, take the "green lane" bridleway on the right going east to the bridleway which comes due north from Woodstock. Cross dogleggedly into the "green lane" opposite which leads southeast back to the start.

<u>Alternative routes.</u> Within this route, nine other bridleways offer many variations, e.g.:-

THE DORN VALLEY CIRCUIT, 9 miles (15 km) which joins Points 3 and 10 and which can also be started from Church Lane, Steeple Barton.

Leave **Barton Abbey Park** (Point 3) and turn left along the minor road. Go down to the River Dorn and then up to the cross roads at Church Farm, **Steeple Barton** (800 m). Turn sharp left, into Church Lane which is, first a green lane bridleway going south and then, after 2 miles, becomes a field bridleway dropping gently down into low-lying fields in the Dorn valley bottom. Here the bridleway from the Church arrives in **"Purgatory"** at an isolated barn (recalling Bunyan's *"Pilgrim's Progress"* and Dante's *"La divina commedia").* Continue south to a gated farm track on the east side of Bushwell's Thicket and exit onto a minor road at Tittenford Bridge west of Point 2. Turn right and then immediately fork left, riding south east for 2.5 km along a minor road (good verges) past **Woottondown Fm** to the B4027 cross-roads at **Wootton** (Point 10). [1]

Route 1:-The DORN VALLEY and GREAT TEW

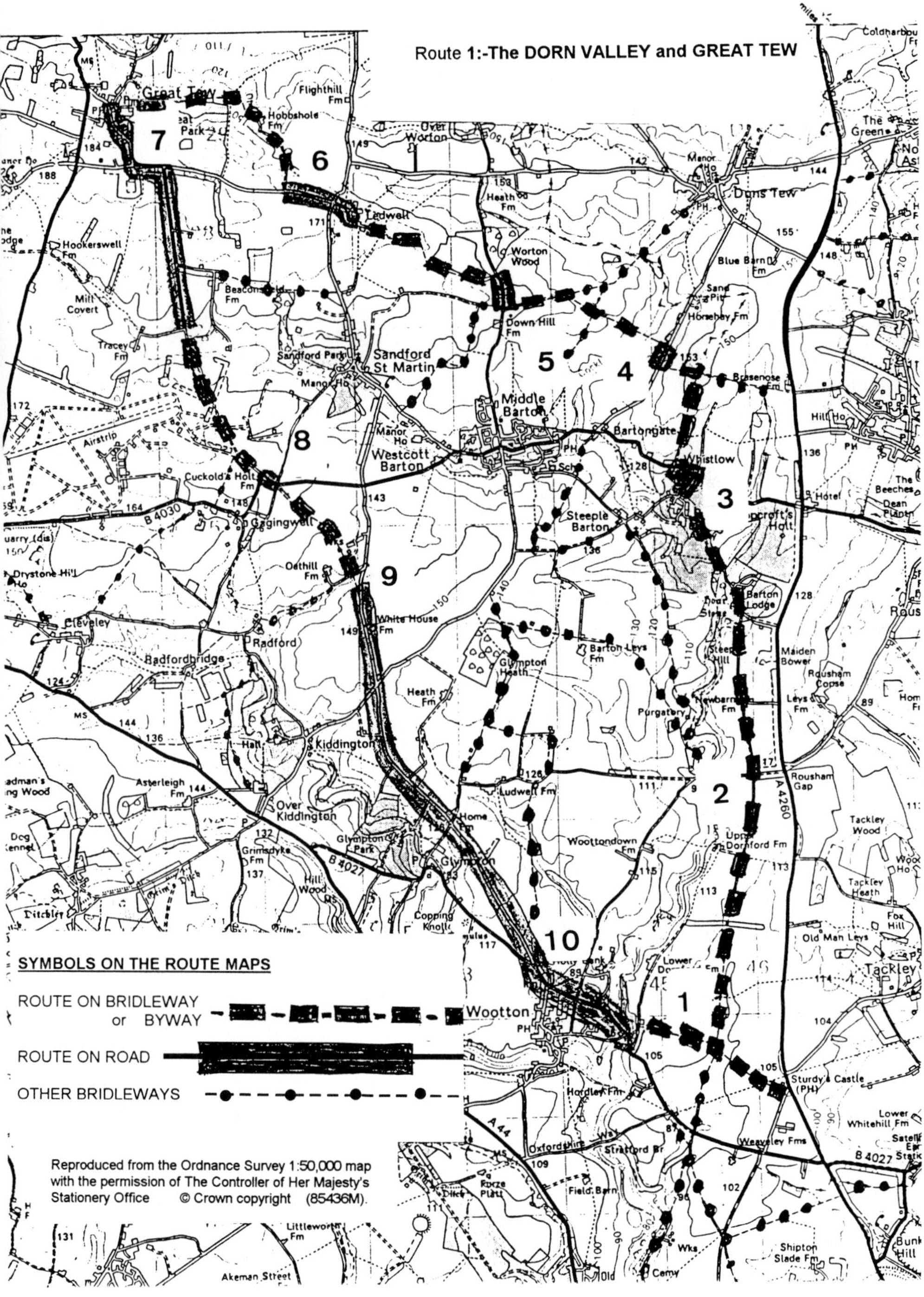

SYMBOLS ON THE ROUTE MAPS

ROUTE ON BRIDLEWAY or BYWAY

ROUTE ON ROAD

OTHER BRIDLEWAYS

Route 2:- BICESTER to COTTISFORD

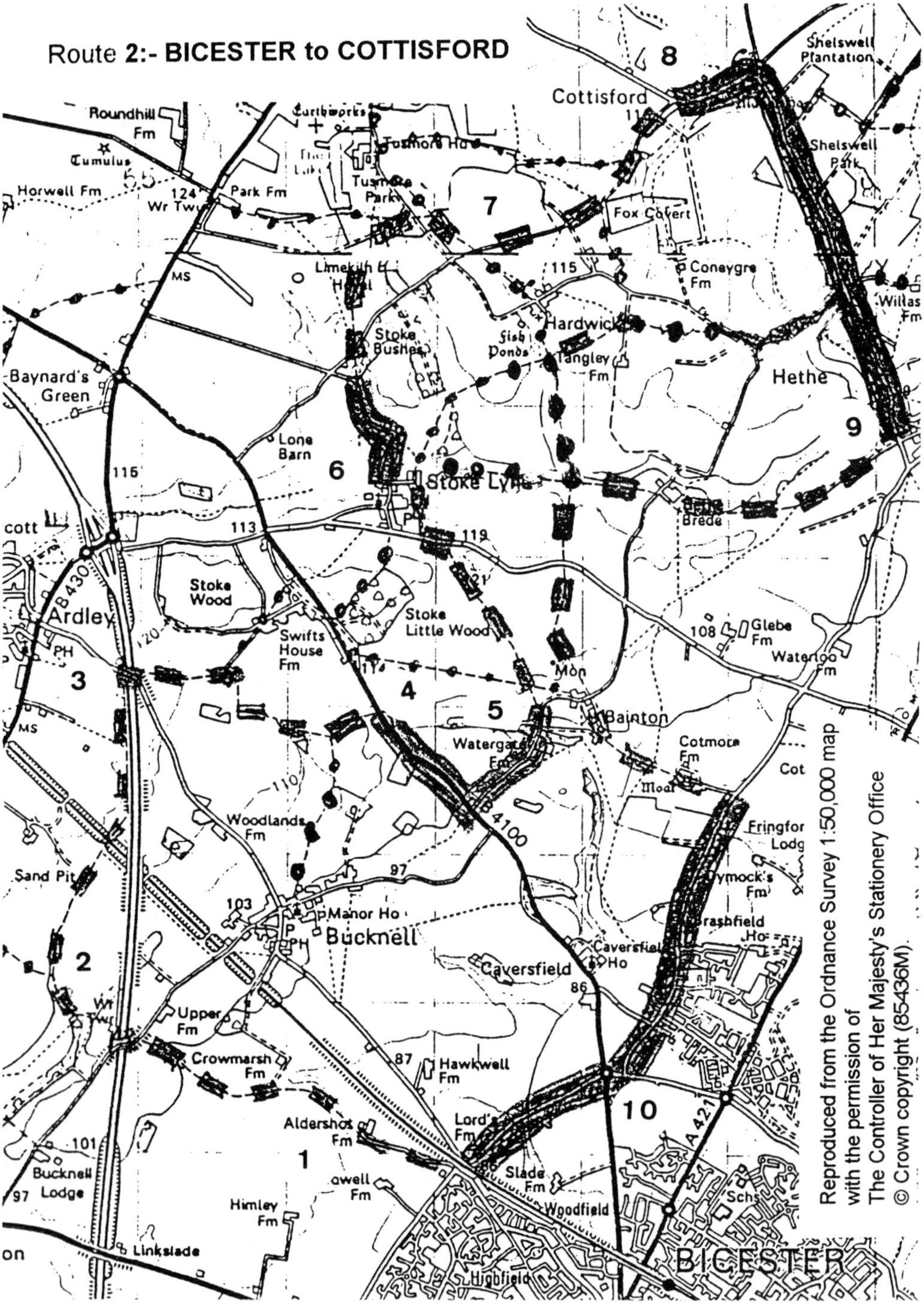

.BICESTER north to COTTISFORD Route 2

14 miles, circular (clockwise)
Ordnance Survey maps:
Landranger 164 and 152
Pathfinder 1069 and 1045
Length:
14 miles (23 km) in total, of which
9.5 miles (15 km) bridleway.
Several shorter alternatives.
Parking & starting point
a) Aldershot Fm. road, Bicester; Mr.Derek Ricketts (tel.01869 25366).(GR.565241)
b) Waterloo Farm (Mrs. Phillippa Taylor, tel.01869 277241) and Laurels Farm (Mrs. R. Wise, tel.01869 277250) on the road Fringford to Bicester. (Plse. phone first).

Route description:-

1. From Aldershot Fm., take the field-edge bridleway north west for two fields, then as an across-fields bridleway for two fields going west. Continue northwest across two more fields, heading for the by the M40. Turn left at a minor road (Bucknell to Middleton Stoney), go over the motorway and then immediately turn right into the **Wt Twr** service road (GR.549248). Take the "green lane" bridleway into and along Gaggle Brook for 20 m between a wood and "Trow Pool".

2. Turn right, then right, entering a field bridleway, going north, along a left hand hedge and then, over a ditch, along a right hand hedge. Go past **Ardley Sand pit** and quarry, now an O.C.C. refuse disposal site. Cross the single track railway line (CARE) and continue to the M40 boundary fence. Turn left, north, along the fence for four fields to the Ardley to Bucknell road.

3. Turn right over the M40 bridge and then immediately on the other side, turn left along a concrete farm track bridleway going east towards **Swift's House**. After 600 m turn off right at Kilby's Barn, and go south onto a field-edge bridleway which then goes east dogleggedly to a hunting gate on the B4100 (GR.566269).

4. Cross (CARE) onto the wide verge on the opposite side and turn right, going south east for 900 m. to Watergate Lodge on the corner of a minor lane. Turn left to the ford at **Watergate Farm**.

5. Where the road bends right at **Bainton,** turn left into a field bridleway, follow the right-hand hedge to the corner gate and bridge over a ditch into the next field. Turn left north west on a fieldedge track and then a crossfield bridleway, (1.1 km) to a minor road (Stoke Lyne to Stratton Audley). Turn left along the road for 200 m and then turn right on the farm track bridleway going north across two fields to an unmetalled lane. Turn left to Lower Farm, **Stoke Lyne** *(the "Wykham Arms" PH is on your left).*

6. Turn right going north for 1 km. along a minor road (Stoke Lyne to Hardwick). Enter a bridleway, into Stoke Bushes on your right, cross a minor road to enter a cross-field bridleway going due north then north east (1 km) into **Tusmore Park** (*This well-run estate is noted for its pheasant shooting and an elegant 18th. century house near the site of an abandoned 14th century village*). Turn right east for 300m. and enter wooden double gates into parkland. Bear right to wooden gates at the south end of "*Lime Avenue*" and enter "*Yew Avenue*" going south east for 400 m.

7. Turn left east onto a "green lane" track, "*Buckingham Lane*" along the southern edge of Tusmore Wood, which leads north

east to **Fox Covert** and then to College Fm., **Cottisford** *(Called "Fordlow" in Flora Thompson's "Lark Rise", 1939).*

8. Turn right, ride past the Church and the Manor, then turn right again at the road junction (600 m). Go by road (verge for 1.5 km) to the **Hethe** "T" road junction and continue on for 1 km to the first "T" road junction at **Fringford** *(Turn left then right to the "The Butcher's Arms" PH on the village green which Flora Thompson called "Candleford Green", 1943).*

9. Turn right, southwest on a farm track to Hollow Barn and then west across fields (boggy) to **Hethe Brede Fm.** Cross the road onto a field edge bridleway to Hardwick Ford. Turn left, due south, for two fields; recross the Stoke Lyne/Stratton Audley road (CARE this is a blind corner on a narrow road) (GR.578279). Follow the field edge bridleway past Thornton's Barn ruin *(a 19C. Bicester MP and MFH erected the mid-field monument on your right in memory of a favorite bitch)* to **Bainton**. Enter the signposted bridleway opposite through Home Fm. yard into fields (often boggy) bearing east to **Cotmore Fm** "Moat Fm." Turn right along the Fringford to Bicester road (GR.591264).

10. Continue south past South Lodge Riding School (Parking; tel. 01869 2439340) to the "T" road junction at the new housing ahead at **Bicester**. Turn right and cross the B4100 roundabout (CARE) into the road opposite (good verge). At the railwaybridge mini roundabout (1 km), turn left, then immediately right, along the track back to **Aldershot Fm.** (600 m).

Alternative routes

11(A). In wet conditions, at the "T" road-junction, on the Cottisford to Fringford road (para.8 above), turn down to **Hethe**. After the stream, the village well & war memorial, the church and the *"The Whitmore Arms"* PH (tel.01869 277363), bear left at the fork, down the road (verge) to **Hethe Brede Fm.** and up to the Stoke Lyne cross roads. Turn left, east towards Stratton Audley and at the next cross roads, turn right, south, along the road past "Moat Fm." to **Bicester** (see para. 10).

11(B). At **Hethe** after the PH, fork right, west, towards Hardwick. After the houses, turn left onto a fieldedge bridleway going behind allotments. First cross a field, then the **Tangley Fm.** track and continue south east diagonally across a further field. Follow the righthand hedge to a coppice and fish ponds where a bridleway from the Church at **Hardwick** (O.E. *"Herd Farm"*) comes in from your right (GR.578293) (1.2 km). Turn left for 1 field, going down to the hunting gate at Hardwick Ford and after the ford, either continue due south (see para. 9) or turn right, due west, to Lower Fm., Stoke Lyne and retrace your route to Bainton (see para. 5 above). [1]

MASTER OF THE HOUNDS.

19 miles, circular (anti-clockwise)
Ordnance Survey maps:
Landranger 164
Pathfinder 1092, 1116, 1093 and 1117
Length:
19 miles (30 km) in total, of which
13 miles (21 km) bridleway.
N.B. Winter floods and MoD. Rifle Range (tel. 01865 716060).

Parking (verges) **& starting points**
(i) opp. Folly Farm, Common La., Beckley; (ii) verge opposite New Inn Farm on B4027 (at point 2) (iii) "*Ragnall's Lane*", Horton - cum-Studley (GR.590125).

Route description

1. *(Common Lane on the Oxford Heights,* GR55711, *provides splendid views over the Otmoor fenland 60m. lower*). Take Common Lane east into **Beckley** (*formerly the administrative centre for the seven "towns" of medieval Otmoor*) passing the lynch-gated church on your left and turn right to the "*Abingdon Arms*" PH. Turn right, going due south along "Roman Way" then enter a bridleway track "Sandy Lane" (*this Roman road runs north/south between Roman Dorchester and Alcester, close to the modern military base at Bicester*). Cross over New Inn Road, by the radio/TV mast which is your most prominant land mark for today, into a field bridleway between two barbed-wire fences, passing to the east of **Stow Wood**.

2. At the B4027, exit (CARE) by **New Inn Fm** and turn right along the wide verge opposite for 100m. Turn left on a bridleway track to continue south for 6 fields. Before a spinney, turn right into **Wick Farm** and caravan park (*the Well on your right is Roman)*.

3. Go down the farm road to **Barton,** over Bayswater Brook, follow the road right, then take the first road left, going east through housing for 1 km. Cross the busy road (Horton to Headington) into Waynflete Road almost opposite. Ride up the hill for 500 m to the first left turn (marked Bayswater Fm.).

4. Take a narrow bridleway going east between fields and gardens at **Sandhills**. After a play area, continue through fields, cross the brook, climb slightly, then steeply, to exit beside the Chapel at **Forest Hill**. Turn left for 200 m.

5. Cross the B4027 (CARE) to the "*White Horse*" PH. (tel.01865 873927) and enter "*Polecat Lane*", a green lane bridleway, going north east to a bridge at Moorbirge Brook (GR.597086) and a field bridleway at the **Polecat End of Waterperry Wood.**

6. <u>Choose 6 (A) or 6 (B</u>) Alternative routes round Waterperry Wood to Menmarsh Corner.

6 (A) Go left, taking the field bridleway for 1.km to a field gate leads into a farm track going due north or

6 (B) Go right, taking the field bridleway which goes for 1.5 km east to **Drunkard's Corner**. Enter a green lane bridleway going north east for 1.5 km, then turn left on a minor road (2 km.) south of Bernwood Forest *(on OS map as* ***"Shabbington Wood"****, a former Royal Deer Forest, & now a Forestry Nature Reserve famous for butterflies and grazing deer*).

7. At **Menmarsh guide post** road junction (GR.602103), take the surfaced farm road to "**Danesbrook Fm**". Passing the farm and buildings to your left, turn west then north to **Stanton Little Wood** and cross two fields and a small wooden bridge to join a minor road. Turn right along the road for 700 m.

8. At **Horton-cum-Studley** turn left by the *Victorian* Church of St. Barnabas into Mill Lane (GR.593125). Before **West Hill Fm.**, fork right into a bridleway track ("*Ragnall's Lane*") which leads northwest to a gate onto **Otmoor** at "100 Acre Field" (GR.581144). A red flag warns if crossing is unsafe because of firing at the MoD's **Rifle range** to the south; (rifle practice may be held any day except Tuesdays or Thursdays and some holidays; tel. MoD).

Choose alternative route 9 (if there is NO firing) or 10 (if there IS firing practice)

9. If safe to cross "100 Acre Field" Enter Otmoor going west for 800 m. to a set of wooden gates (GR.572145) (route Point 11) which mark the bridleway going N/S Alcester to Dorchester on the *Roman Road* and which offer choice of alternatives 9 (a), or 9 (b):-

9 (a) Go due south heading for the TV mast at Beckley. Cross a dyke (over a gated bridge) and continue to a hunting gate (GR.572129) south west of the Butts which leads to a bridleway on the embankment (route Point 14). Instead of going due west to **Noke**, turn immediately left into a green lane leading due south onto a metalled lane which rises up to **Beckley.**

9 (b) Go due west for 1.5 km on a degraded green lane track, past the Joseph's Stone, towards **Oddington** (this lane can flood deeply in winter). Before & below the village, turn south at the New River Ray bridge (route Point 12) using, first a farm road then, a field track bridleway to **Lower Fm.**, **Noke** (2 km). Turn left, eastwards, and continue on a raised embankment to the south west corner of "100 Acre Field" by the Butts (route Point 14). By-pass the hunting gate and turn right into a green lane bridleway and then a metalled lane which rises up to **Beckley** village.

10. If NOT safe to cross "100 Acre Field Retreat 1 km along "Ragnall's Lane", turn left along a farm track bridleway (GR.586137) which goes north and north east to Manor Farm, **Whitecross Green** (Point 15). Turn left along the road through **Murcott** ("*The Nut Tree*" *PH with hitching ties at the back, tel.* 01865 331253). Just before **Fencott,** take a green lane on your left to re-enter Otmoor (route Point 17). If you continue straight ahead on the north/south *Roman road* bridleway, (ignoring a green lane bridleway on your right), a second MoD flagpole will indicate whether it is safe to continue south to the wooden gates at the entrance to "100 Acre Field" (route Point 11)

Choose alternatives 10 (a) 10 (b) or 10 (c).

10 (a) If no red flag flies, go due south heading for the TV mast at **Beckley** and follow the route described in para. 9 (a).

10 (b) If a red flag is flying here also, turn back to the green lane bridleway (now on your left) which leads west and then north into **Charlton on Otmoor** (this lane can flood in winter). At the PH, (route Point 19) turn left and continue by road to **Oddington**. At the village green, turn left down a green lane to re-enter Otmoor. (*The 13C church has the grave of Maori princess Papakura who lived in the village until her death in 1930 and of five Maori soldiers who died in WWI*). At the New River Ray bridge (route Point 12), turn right along a farm road then a grass track which goes south to **Lower Fm., Noke** and then east to the Butts (route Point 14). See last sentence in para. 9 (b).

10 (c) If the green lane in para.10 (b) is flooded, continue by road (Point 17) via **Fencott** to **Charlton-on-Otmoor** and **Oddington.** [1]

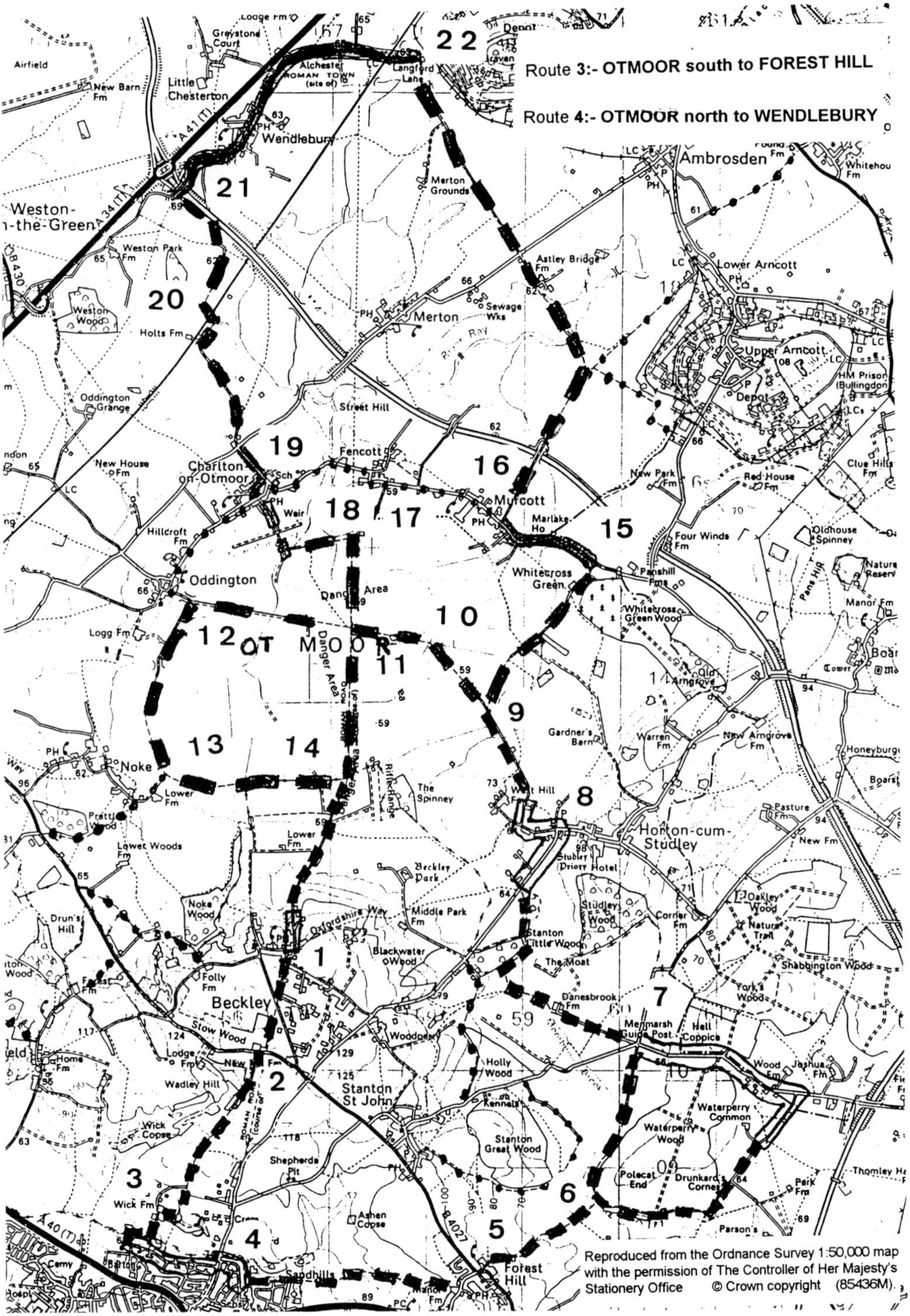

Route **3**:- **OTMOOR south to FOREST HILL**

Route **4**:- **OTMOOR north to WENDLEBURY**

OTMOOR north to WENDLEBURY Route 4

19 miles, circular, (clockwise)
Ordnance Survey maps:
Landranger 164
Pathfinder 1092, 1092
Length:
16 miles (26 km) in total, of which
13 miles (21 km) bridleway.
N.B. Winter floods and MoD. Rifle Range (Tel.01865 716060)

Parking & starting points
(i) Wendlebury Gate Stables, Langford Lane, Merton (Hazel Offord tel. 01869 252224) (GR.578203)
(ii) "*The Nut Tree*" PH Murcott. (plse. first tel. 01865 331253) Parking & hitching rail
(iii) "*Ragnall's Lane*", Horton-cum-Studley (GR.590125).

Route description

1. From the Wendlebury Gate Stables (route Point 22, approached from Bicester), take the farm track bridleway going due south, then south east. Cross the minor Merton-to-Ambrosden road at **Astley Bridge Fm.** (GR.589183). Go south of the farm through a field to rejoin the farm track, which crosses the River Ray curving south and then south west to the M40. Climb a long, steep farm bridge with high parapets over the M40 and continue along the track "*Field Lane*" to **Murcott** where "*The Nut Tree*" PH is just to your right *(You are only 59m. above sea level)* (Point 16).

2. <u>Choose alternative 2-(a) or 2-(b)</u> to avoid rifle practice and/or winter floods on Otmoor. At four entry points to the MoD. danger area, GR.568145, GR.572130, GR.572147 & GR.581144, there are flagpoles where red flags are flown to warn when rifle practice takes place *[this can be any day except Tues. or Thurs. so phone the MOD]*. Use Beckley radio/TV mast for compass bearings.

2-(a) Go right, west, on a minor road through **Murcott** and **Fencott** to **Charlton-on-Otmoor** (route Point 19) *(this route avoids floods).*

2-(b) Go right, west, through **Murcott** but, before **Fencott,** take a green lane bridleway on your left (route Point 17) which goes south west between enclosed fields. Then turn right at a bridleway fork, (Point 18) and go west then north west to **Charlton-on-Otmoor** *(this route avoids Otmoor rifle practice)*.

3. <u>To reach the open fens of **Otmoor,** choose alternative 3 (a) or 3 (b).</u>

3 (a) At route Point 18, continue due south, on the *Roman road* bridleway to wooden gates at the NW corner of the "100 Acre" Field (route Point 11).

3 (b) Go left east, along a minor road. At **Whitecross Green** by the Manor Farm entrance (1 km), turn right onto a farm track bridleway leading southwest to "*Ragnall's Lane*"(1.9 km) (route Point 9). Turn right north west to a metal field gate and enter Otmoor at the north east corner of the "100 Acre Field". Go due west for 800 m to a set of wooden gates (GR.572145) (route Point 11).

4. <u>Choose alternatives 4(a), 4(b) or 4(c)</u>

4 (a) Go due south *(across the land used pre-war for RAF bombing practice ; hence the water-filled pits in winter*). South west of the Butts, a hunting gate (GR.572129) (route Point 14) leads to a bridleway on the embankment going due west to **Noke**. (*Noke was the last of the seven "towns" of Otmoor to be cleared of forest, the last to be the subject of a commons enclosure order by Parliament in 1830 and the area of the most recent*

land reclamation by drainage in the 1960s). Turn north to **Oddington**, then east to return to the wooden gates (a *7 km route circuiting wild fenland of natural and scientific interest*).

4 (b) Go due W. past Jacob's Stone on a degraded bridleway track (severe winter floods) which rises up into **Oddington** (1.5 km). *(Detour left to a delightful church with strong Maori connections having: the grave of a Maori princess married to a local farmer, a Maori grass skirt and a wooden carving to five Maori soldiers killed in World War I*). Turn right and go north by road to **Charlton-on-Otmoor** (1.5 km).

4 (c) Go due north along an improved green lane (*the N/S Roman road to Alcester*). At 900 m, turn left (route Point 18) into a degraded green lane bridleway (winter floods) going west and then north to **Charlton-on-Otmoor** (1.3 km). If this bridleway is flooded, turn right north east to **Fencott** (600 m). At the road turn left west to **Charlton-on-Otmoor** (1.5 km).

5. At **Charlton on Otmoor**, opposite "*The Crown*" PH (tel 01867.833237), (route Point 19) take Church Road and head north west for 600 m to the "T" junction by Home Farm (GR.560163) on the minor Islip to Merton road.

6. Take the green lane bridleway opposite, ("*Mansmoor Road*") going north west towards the farm buildings at **Holt's Fm**. (route Point 20). Before the railway level crossing (1.3 km), take a gate on the right (GR.556174) into a green lane leading to a second railway crossing some 300 m to the east. Cross the railway line (CARE at the double gates). Pass through a BBONT scientific site *(Bucks, Berks & Oxon Nature Trust*) and follow the right-hand hedge to a concrete farm track which runs up to, then alongside, the M40 (past a former pit now a waste disposal site).

7. At the minor road, turn right and cross the M40 on a low-parapet bridge shared with vehicules (route Point 21). Continue by road through **Wendlebury** ("*The Red Lion*" PH tel. 01869.252514) and return to Langford Lane (3.7 km).[1]

14 Riding Pillion

A Medieval Chapman

18 miles, circular (anti-clockwise)
Ordnance Survey maps:
Landranger 164, 151 & 152
Pathfinder 1069, 1045
Length:
18 miles (29 km) in total, of which
13 miles (21 km) bridleway.
Two shorter alternatives
Parking & starting points
(i) road verges, Somerton to Fritwell road (GR.512291);
(ii) cross roads 1.5 km south of Hinton in the Hedges (GR.556357);
(iii) "*The Bear*" PH, Souldern (tel.01869 346785) (GR.527312).
Route description

1. Take the road into **Fritwell** (O.E. "*Wishing well*"). You pass on the right St. Olaf's 11 Cent. Church with two Norman doorways opposite a Grade-I listed Jacobean Manor House, *(linked to three tragedies & reputedly haunted. Sir John Simon, Home Secretary, Chancellor of the Exchequer and Foreign Secretary during the "Baldwin appeasement years" lived here in the 1930s.).* At the cross roads, continue ahead on a minor road which goes over the M40 to a "T" junction with the B4100 (good visibility).

2. Cross the B4100 (CARE) into the green lane bridleway opposite which leads into a field-edge path. By **Tower Farm,** cross over a minor road onto a field bridleway going due north with right hand hedges to a narrow gated bridge across Ockley Brook. Follow left-hand hedges due north across five gated fields down to a track into **Croughton** (2 km). At the brook, turn left into a steep field and go north west across two small paddocks to the B4031.

3. Cross the B4031 (CARE, but visibility good) into the minor road opposite. Go north then west for 1.5 km to a "T" road-junction (Ayhno to **Charlton**, GR.533345).

4. Take the field bridleway by the plantation on your right for 2.5 km. It goes north, then north east into a green lane and leads to a minor road (Charlton to Evenley).

5. Turn right by road for 500 m to a crossroads with shaded parking on wide verges. Turn left going north by road for 1.5 km to **Hinton-in-the-Hedges** village. Pass the PH. and bear left to a right-angle bend in the road.

6. Continue north west for 2.4 km along a gated road past **Steane Grounds Farm**, to a minor road to the Airfield. Enter the green lane opposite, still bearing north west, and then cross a second minor road (from Charlton to Farthinghoe) just south of **Farthinghoe Lodge** into "Sandy Lane", a green lane which goes west dropping down to open fields (1 km).

7. Turn right north along a field-edge bridleway towards **Great Purston Manor House** (1.5 km). Then double back south west along the estate road, between the manor house and barns. Where the estate road bends north to **Little Purston**, take a field bridleway on your left. Before **Buston Fm.**, turn sharp left in the third field and climb steeply uphill to a hunting gate in the top corner. Go due south to **Astrophill Fm**.

8. Turn left at the farm track for 250 m to join, below the wood at **Rosamund's Bower**, a bridleway on the right which goes diagonally down one field between electric fencing and along two right hand hedges to **Upper Astrop Park Fm**. Go left, by road for 1 km south to **King's Sutton**. At the village, take the first residential road left, to a minor road coming from Charlton.

Route 5:- FRITWELL, HINTON-in the HEDGES and AYHNO

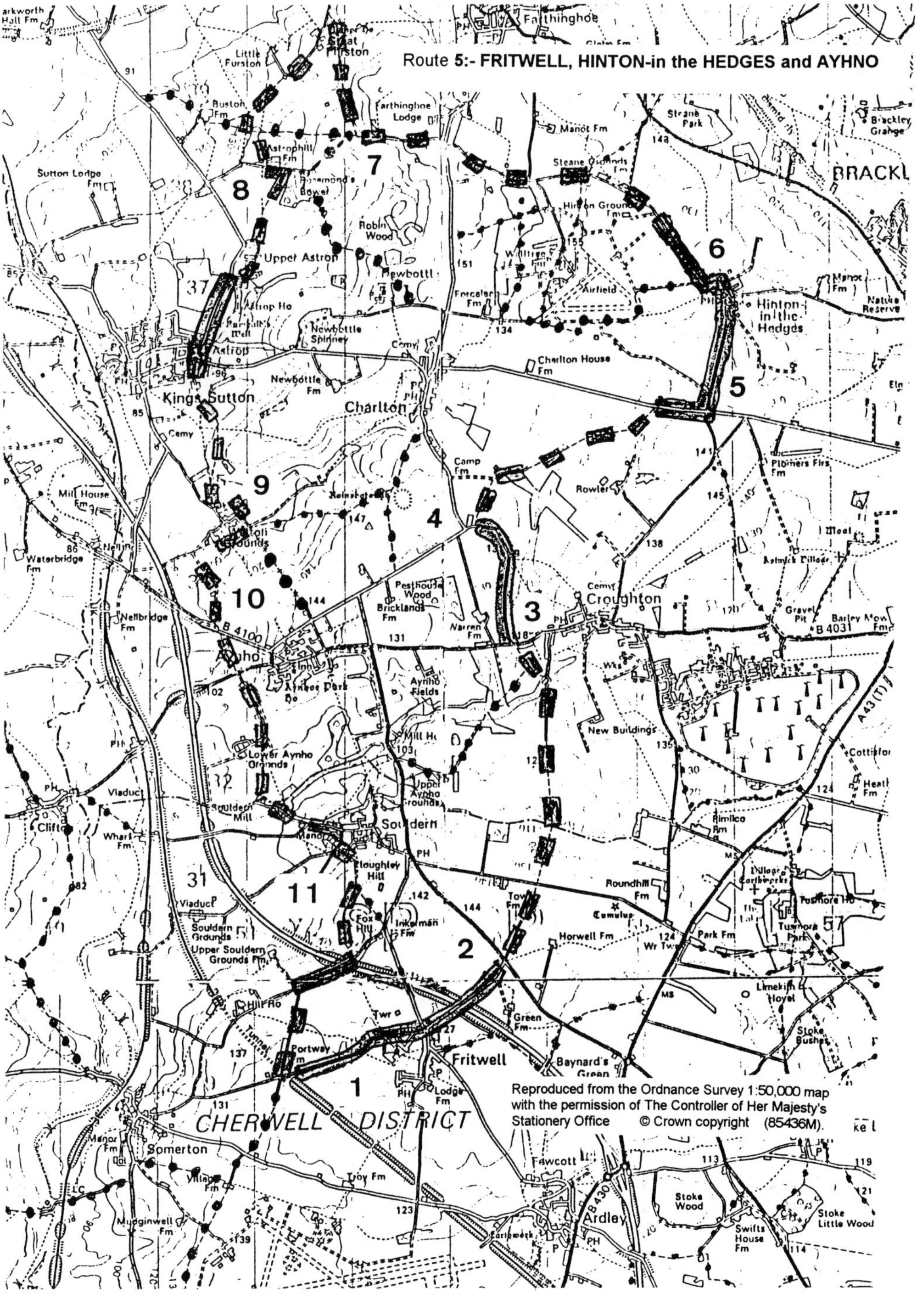

(*Two PH.s, "The Bell" and "The White Horse" are only 500m. to your right near the church).* Cross over the road diagonally left, into a lane, which ends in a farm yard leading to a field bridleway down to a brook. Follow the left hedge until the bridleway climbs, diagonally right across the field to the top right hand corner. In the next field, pass by a small covert. Continue due south diagonally across one field & along a second fieldhedge to farm cottages at **Walton Grounds** (1.5 km).

9. Turn left then right (100 m), into one field, going left to a gate into a second field. Take a bridge over the stream, to a field bridleway crossroads (100 m). The lefthand path goes east to Charlton; the one opposite goes southwards as a green lane up to **Aynho** (*DB. 1086 "Aega's hill"*). Turn right, westwards, and go through two fields skirting round Walton Grounds Farm which is now *Twyfords Seeds Research* buildings. Follow the concrete farm road which heads for the M40 ahead, but turns left up, and then down, to the B4100.

10. Turn left along the layby for 150 m and cross the B4100 (CARE) into the field bridleway opposite. Follow the left-hand hedge across a brook to a green lane. Cross the B4301 (CARE) onto a macadam farm road directly opposite. Continue below the grounds of **Aynho House** *(17th Cent. Palladian with a Vanbrugh-style Church built in 1723)* south along the farm road (until it curves away right into **Lower Ayhno Grounds Farm**). Follow the farm track, here with twin concrete strips, down to the ford at **Souldern Mill**. and up to the quiet, well-kept beauty of **Souldern** village *(OE "Sulethorne" or thorn tree in a gulley),* past the **Manor** Ho. (*with splendid wrought-iron gates*) and *"The Fox"* PH (tel.01869 345284).

11. Take the road on your right ("Fox Lane") leading south past **Ploughley Hill** to a green lane bridleway. Fork right to **Fox Hill** and Fox Hill Barn. Exit onto a minor road (Souldern to Somerton) and turn right. Cross over the M40 and after 300 m turn left into a green lane bridleway, to return along a secondary roman road (*The Portway*) past **Portway Fm.** to the start.

Alternative routes:-

(A) At Point 4, go by road, past **Camp Fm.** to **Charlton.** The field bridleway on your left before the stream, rises south west towards *Rainsborough Camp.* Below this *Camp,* where the field bridleways fork, turn right downhill to **Walton Grounds**, Aynho at Point 9.
Then go either:-
A (1) south to Aynho and Points 10 & 11 and return to the Start, or
A (2) north to Kings Sutton and Points 8, 7, 6 & 5. Both are 11 miles in length.

(B) At Point 6, go west on a fieldedge bridleway on your left. Edging round the Airfield to a minor road near **Forceleap Fm**. Cross a minor road (from Farthinghoe to Charlton) and continue west towards **Newbottle** but before this hamlet, turn off at a wood on your right. A field bridleway, which goes north then west, drops down to a stream before climbing north-west up to **Rosamond's Bower** at Point 8.[1]

HEYTHROP, DITCHLEY and the GLYME VALLEY Route 6

21 miles, circular (clockwise)

Ordnance Survey maps:
Landranger 164,
Pathfinder 1068, 1069, 1091

Length:
21 miles (33 km) in total, of which
13 miles (20 km) bridleway.
One safe, shorter alternative.

Parking & starting points
(a) verge, Callow Farm, 1 km due north of Stonesfield (GR.395182).
(b) layby, Chalford Green (GR.342246).
(c) verge, west of Heythrop (GR.345280).

Route description

1. Take a green lane going north west from **Callow Fm**. (this BOAT continues for 7 km to Chipping Norton). Ride through 3 fields with gates, crossing over, first a bridleway (from Ditchley to Stonesfield) and then the B4437 into another green lane which later becomes a farm track. Continue past Dustfield Farm and the Lodge gates of **Ditchley Park**. (*with an 18 C Model farm besides Grim's Ditch. The mansion, designed by James Gibbs, used as Churchill's weekend HQ in WW2, is now an Anglo-American conference centre*).

2. Just after **Norman's Grove**, where the track forks left, continue straight ahead, north west. Cross (CARE) over the B4022 Enstone to Charlbury road, then over a minor road from Enstone to Splelsbury. Exit at the B4026 Spelsbury to Chipping Norton road (GR.353236).

Choose either:- 3(A) or 3(B)

3(A) Take the road north west for 1 mile to **Chalford Green**. After the fork coming from Lidstone, take the green lane BOAT at the layby on your right and go down into the Glyme valley to the Golf course.

3(B) Take the cross-field bridleway on your right for one field, turn right going through and then along one hedgerow past the Trig. point (187 m). Cross a minor road into a bridleway for two fields to **Lidstone**. Turn left along Stone Farm road and continue on a field bridleway north west to **Old Chalford Fm**. Take a farm track going down north between two lakes on the River Glyme. Enter a steep field on your left, where the bridleway goes west to a ford. Turn right up the valley to rejoin the BOAT just before the golf course.

4. Continue north west past the golf course on your right, through two gates at New Chalford Farm to the London Road, **Chipping Norton**. (GR.334260). Cross (CARE) into the green lane opposite going north for 500 m to the very busy A44 Oxford to Stratford on Avon road. Cross (CARE) into a minor road (some verges) which winds round eastwards to **Heythrop** (*a model village built in 1873 with damp courses, underground water storage tanks and outside closets*) and a magnificant avenue of trees and then northwards past **Dunthrop Fm**.

5. At the "T" road-junction, turn east along the minor road for about 1 mile. Turn left onto a farm track bridleway towards **Magpie Fm**. After the first field gate, turn off north east on a cross-field bridleway and drop down to a ford and a green lane leading to **Little Tew.** Turn right along the road and keep bearing left through the village. Cross over the B4022 (CARE) and go east to Ledwell. (The second turn left goes down to **Great Tew** with thatched cottages and the only possible break at "*The Falkland Arms*" PH or the rebuilt post office cum shop).

6. Take the first turn right, opposite the parkland, and go due south along a metalled farm road (to **Beaconsfield & Tracy Fms**.) which becomes a track bridleway down to Poor Bridge and Ford. Continue south east to a spinney, then turn left to **Cuckold's Halt Farm** (GR.410256). Join the B4030 and go east for 100 m (verge) to the Sandford St. Martin road junction. Take the bridleway opposite, going through double gates, south along a right-hand hedge for two fields by **Gagingwell**.

7. Turn left along a minor road to the farm barns at the cross roads. Turn left and then take the first right at Radford Farm down to **Radford Mill**. Behind the wooden stables, take a bridleway rising, first left across the field, and then right along the hedge, to a gate in the corner of the next field which gives access to the plateau. Follow the left-hand hedge due south, through a farm gate into the parkland of **Kiddington Hall.** Follow the track to the farm, going via awkward gates between the double cattle sheds to the estate buildings of Park Fm. Exit right at **Over Kiddington** (GR.411223) onto a minor road for 250 m.

8. Cross the A44 (CARE) onto a minor road leading to **Ditchley.** Turn left to **Grimsdyke Farm** and continue on a farm track going due south. At the spinney entrance to **Out Wood**, take the fieldedge bridleway on your right going south west to a hunting gate. Bear left across the next field, south-south-west down to a narrow spinney where a bridleway crosses at right angles. Drop steeply down the western edge of **Kingswood**; cross a brook (bridge) and turn right along Kingswood Bottom for 150 m. Go left steeply up a green lane, due south, to the B4437. Cross (CARE) into the minor road opposite and return to the start.

A shorter route (18 miles)

At Point 4, turn off the BOAT right, via a bridleway gate onto the golf course. Go east to a bridge over the stream then leave the course on a farm track north east to the very busy A44. Cross (CARE) into the farm track bridleway opposite at **Chalford Oaks Fm** (Point 9).

Go south east to **Broadstone Hill** & Hall. Enter a narrow paddock on your left, turn right and exit by a pond into woods. Cross the stream (bridge) and leave the woods below Talbot Hall in the NatWest Training complex of **Heythrop Hall.** (*The estate was a wedding gift to Albert Brassey from his father, the millionaire surveyor and constructor of railways in five continents. The 18 C Hall, burned to a shell in 1831, was rebuilt by Albert, a local benefactor and keen huntsman, in time to have 1000 dinner guests at the first public meet of the Heythrop Hunt in 1876.*) Turn right, contouring down to recross the stream. Turn left into the next field, traversing up to the corner of the wood whence a track goes through Manor Farm yard. Continue southeast to **Enstone** and exit left onto a back road to **Church Enstone** ("*The Crown*" PH tel. 01608 677262).

Take the lane southeast opposite the church down to the B4022. Cross (CARE) into a field bridleway going past **Drystone Hill House** down to **Cleveley**. Turn left in the village where the bridleway goes east along a lane, over a ford and beside a wood to rise up to minor road which leads east to the crossroads, the farm and the mill at **Radford** (Point 7).

N.B. Five other bridleways which join the very busy A44 between **Chipping Norton** and **Over Kiddington** are NOT recommended.[1]

Route 6:-HEYTHROP, DITCHLEY & the GLYME VALLEY

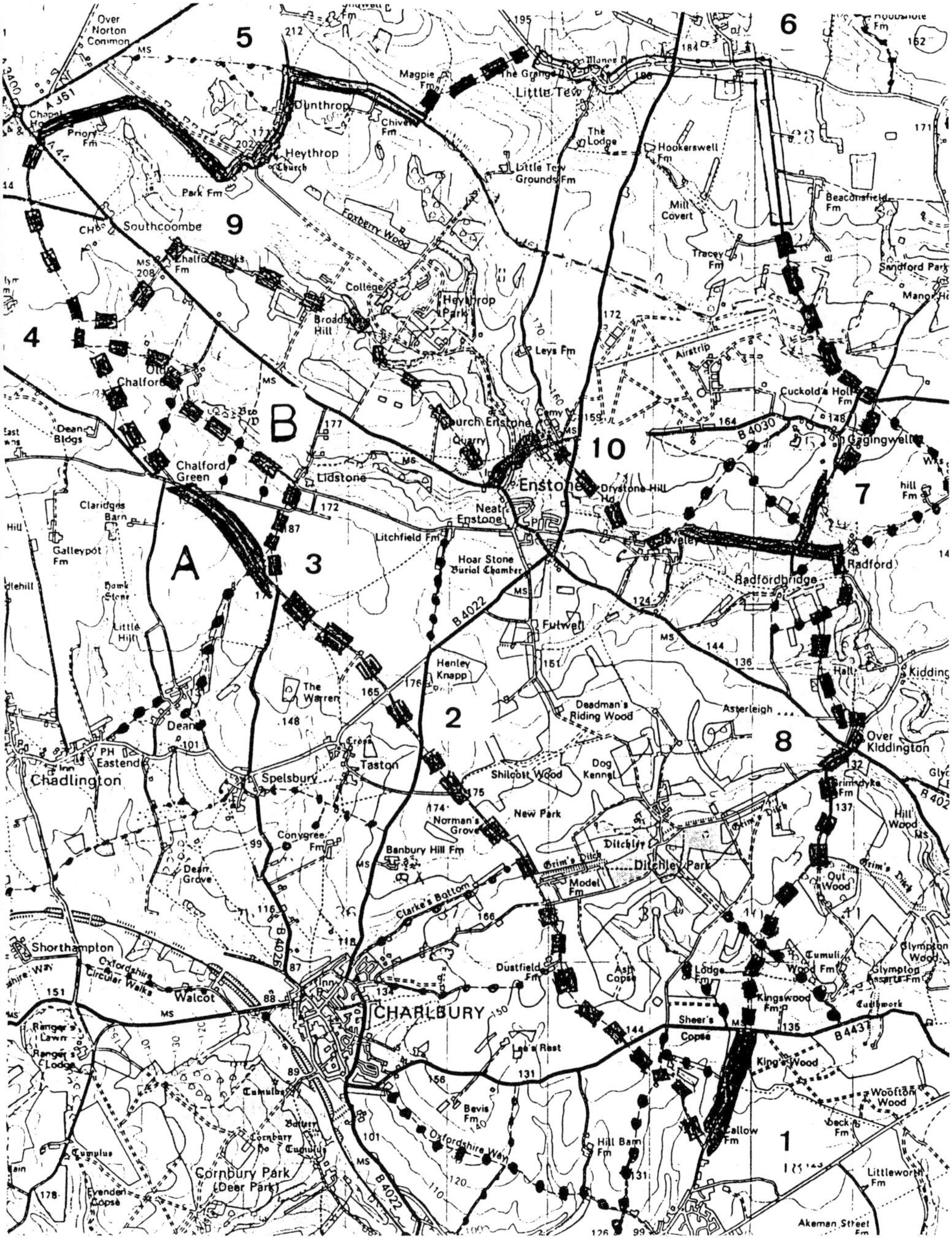

Route 7:-SHELSWELL and STOWE parklands

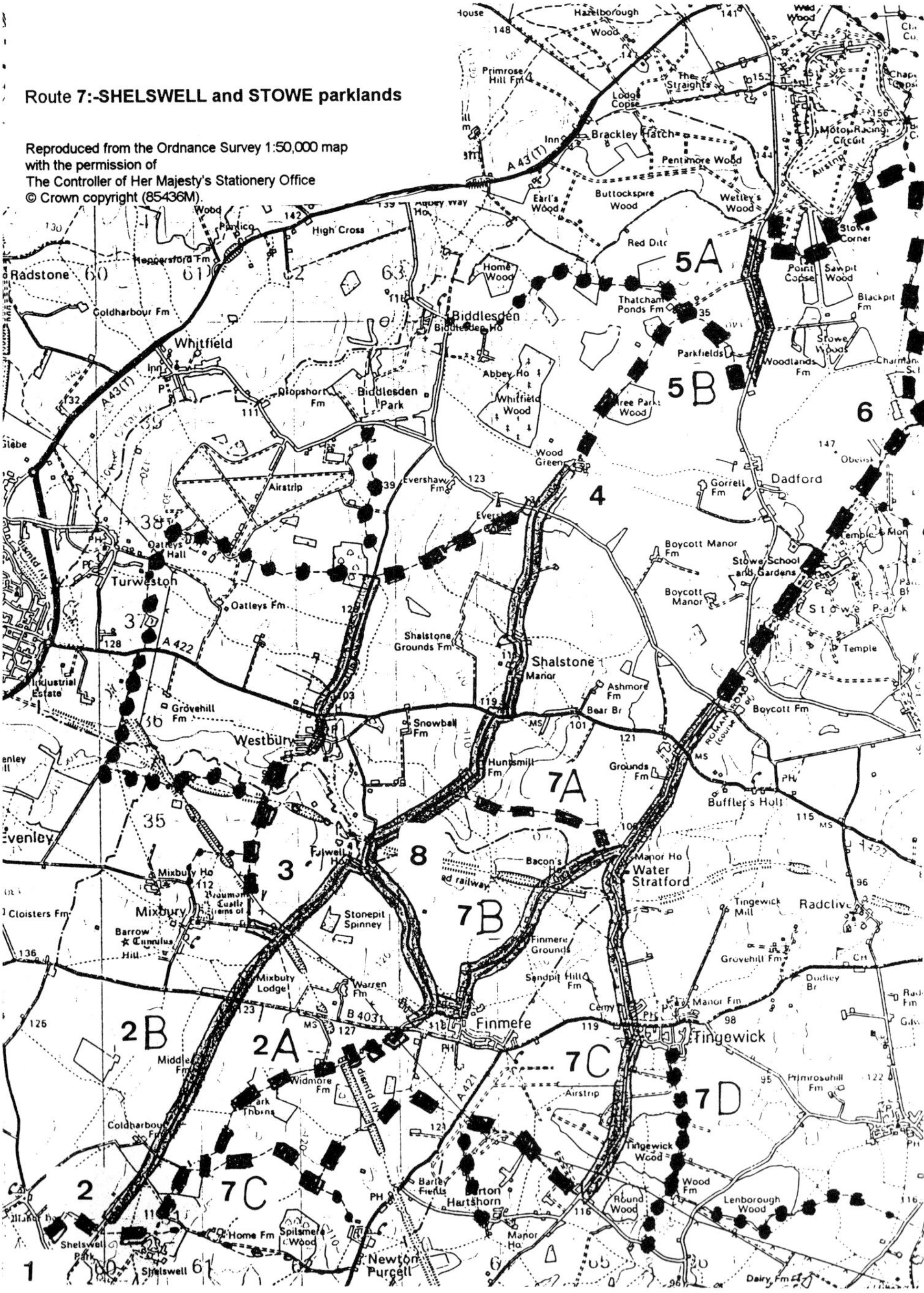

SHELSWELL and STOWE parklands Route 7

23 miles, circular (clockwise)
Ordnance Survey maps:
Landranger 152,
Pathfinder 1045, 1046
Length:
23 miles (37 km) in total, of which
14 miles (23 km) bridleway.

Starting point
Cottisford cross-roads (GR 592312)
Parking:-
(a) road verge, Cottisford/Fringford
(b) Stowe Riding Equestrian Centre, Blackpit Farm, Silverstone Rd. , Stowe, Bucks. tel. 01280 812363; (GR.673398)
(c) Mrs Philippa Taylor, Waterloo Farm, Fringford, plse. tel.01869 277241;
(d) Mrs Wise, Laurels Fm., Fringford, plse. tel.01869 277250.

Route description

1. From the Cottisford to Fringford road take the field-edge bridleway going north east along "The Belt" (GR.593308) (no longer a cross-field path as on OS Pathfinder 1045) then go south east along **Shelswell Plantation** to a minor road.

2. Choose either;- 2(A) or 2(B)

2(A) Take the bridleway opposite across **Shelswell Park**, going dogleggedly northeast, then north, to **Park Thorns** (often a boggy track), **Widmore Fm** and a new quarry with a well-constructed temporary bridleway diversion. Cross the B4031 (CARE) to the lane into **Finmere** village (*O.E. for "woodpeckers' pool*"). Turn left north west along the road to **Fulwell** (GR.627346) (Point 8). Take the first road right (verges) past **Huntsmill Fm**. At the A422 turn right for 100 m (CARE) then turn left onto a minor road (verges) through **Shalstone** village to a cross-roads (GR.644381) (Point 4).

2(B) Turn left along the road on the east side of **Shelswell Plantation**, then along Featherbed Lane, a minor road with good verges, past **Middle Fm.**, to the B4031 and cross (CARE) into the minor road opposite.

3. At a disused railway bridge (Point 3), turn left on the road towards **Mixbury** (DB 1086 "*Misseberie*", O.E. for "*fortified dungheap*"). After 300 m take a field bridleway going north, under a disused railbridge, along a farm track then along a field hedge down to a disused railtrack. Cross a river bridge *(the Great Ouse flows up to Kings Lynn & the Wash*) into a field bridleway to the Mill at **Westbury**. Bear left through the village to the "*The Reindeer*"PH (tel.01280 704934). Cross the A422 (CARE) into the minor road opposite, continuing north. After 1 mile, where a bridleway emerges from the wood on your left ("Ash Furlong Lane") take the field edge bridleway on your right going north east to a brook (bridge & ford) and a spinney which climbs up to **Evershaw Copse**. Exit at a rural road and turn right to cross roads (Point 4) (GR.644381).

4. At the cross roads, take the farm road north to **Wood Green Fm.** and then a field bridleway going north east along an ancient highway *("The Woddeway", a long narrow field)* by **Three Parks Wood** to **Thatcham Ponds Fm.** (2 km). *(The bridleway going west forms part of the Bucks C.C. "Westbury 10 mile Circular Ride" to Biddlesden and Turweston and offers several alternative routes).*

5. Choose 5(A) or 5(B)

5(A) Continue north east along the farm track (an unclassified county road) to a minor road. Turn left for 500 m (verge).

5(B) Turn right opposite the cottages onto a field bridleway going via **Parkfields Fm** to the same road. Turn left for 1.7 km.

Leave the road at **Wetley's Wood** (GR.668410), taking the field-edge bridleway opposite, which goes east, then south round a field with a dirt racing practice track, and east across **Point Copse** and **Sawpit Wood**. (*The Great Riding is usefully aligned with two churches for steeple-chasing and with Wolfe's Obelisk, built eight years before his victory & death on Quebec Heights, which dominates the area from 147 m alt.).* Turn north to the south corner of **Silverstone** racetrack and continue north east on a gravel track with wide grass verges. Then turn east down a hedgerow beside a 4X4 obstacle track. Find a bridleway gate in the bottom corner and turn right, following a field-edge bridleway down to Hoback La. Turn south along a track *(a Roman road from Dorchester, via Bicester, to Towcester*), pass **Home Wood,** continuing south through **Tilehouse Wood** (often boggy) and turn left (gate & jump) into parkland.

6. Turn right along the edge of the wood and exit right by the next gate to a track (GR.685389). (*NB. This section is shown on OS maps 152 and 1023 but omitted from 1046).* Take the track west for 400 m then continue south west for 3 km on a straight *(Roman)* road through **Stowe Park**. *(***Stowe Sch.** *occupies classical 17 C. & 18 C. buildings designed for the Duke of Buckingham whose London house was taken over by George III. and his successors. Set in Wm. Kent's natural landscape,* **Stowe Gardens** *are described by the National Trust as "Britain's largest work of art". This mile long ride, with wide verges and a double avenue of trees, down to the Palladian bridge at* **Oxford Water** *is possibly "Britain's finest bridleway").* Bridlegates by-pass cattle grids at the school entrance and lodge (*named Boycott, after the infamous English land agent of the 1880 Irish famine which led to Gladstone's Land Act 1881*). Cross the A422 (CARE) into the minor road opposite and go to **Water Stratford** by road.

7. <u>Choose either 7(A), 7(B), 7(C)</u>. Please note:- all cross the B4031 or the A421.

7(A). Go west 150 m. down the Finmere road, enter a field bridleway on your right to **Huntsmill Fm.**, turning left southwest by road to **Fulwell** (Point 8). Turn right to Point 3, the B4031 and Featherbed Lane.

7(B). Go south west past **Bacon's Ho**. by road to **Finmere.** Turn right in the village (*about 500 m to the left on the B4031 is "The King's Head" PH tel. 01280 848285)* then second left to the B4031, thence by bridleway to **Widmore Farm** (Point 2A), Thorn Barns and Shelswell Park.

7(C). Go by road south to **Tingewick,** cross (CARE) the A421 into the minor road opposite, going past Aerodrome Farm, to a "T" road-junction. Then turn right into a field bridleway going northwest on former runways. Cross the A421 (with excellent waiting areas both sides) to Finmere Plantation and go southwest along field-edges over a disused railway, then dogleggedly west, back to **Shelswell Park**.

NB. <u>Bypasses</u> of both the B4031 **(Finmere)** and A421 (**Tingewick)** were planned for 1996 with an equestrian bridge over the Tingewick bypass. This will offer access to a 2 km field bridleway route due south on the east side of **Tingewick Wood** followed by a short ride along a minor road to reach the "T" road-junction and runway bridleway mentioned in para. 7(C).[1]

17 miles, circular (anti-clockwise)

Ordnance Survey maps:
Landranger 164,
Pathfinder 1091

Length:
17 miles (27 km) in total, of which
8 miles (13 km) bridleway.

Starting point and Parking:-

Cross roads 1 km north east of Delly End and north west of New Yatt, North Leigh (GR.364138).

Route description

1. Take the lane going east to **Shakeoak Fm** and at 300 m fork right along a green lane bridleway into **North Leigh** (*with its rich tradition of narrative verse:-"They was bad what stole the geese off the common, but they was wuss what stole the comon off the geese" (ref. 1759 Enclosure Award).*

Pass the PH and take the 2nd turning left, a minor road going due north. down the hill to a "T" junction. Turn left, past the new RDA centre and, after 500 m, take a farm track bridleway on your right (GR.386143) down to **Holly Court Fm.**; follow a stream (ford) to **Ashford Bridge** over the **River Evenlode** (1.1 km).

2. Continue north on a minor road, up the hill, turning right over a railway bridge *(Brunel's Oxford, Worcester & Wolverhampton Railway built in 1853).* Cross the Fawler to Stonesfield minor road and enter a farm track bridleway (GR.386173).

3. After 300 m, turn left, west along a farm track bridleway from **Stonesfield** *(The village, famous for frost-split roofing slates, offers a 2 km diversion to a Roman villa, GR.395155. This is a possible picnic site with off-road parking accessible from* **East End.** *A bridleway due south from Stonesfield Church, drops steeply down "The Steps" to the River Evenlode and a deep, gravel-bottomed ford).* At **Hill Barn Farm** Cottages (500 m), the bridleway track continues west, through one field, then another farm track into a spinney which ends at Stonesfield La., **Charlbury.** *(A glovemaking industry, revived by leading Quakers to alleviate poverty resulting from the Napoleonic Wars, survived here until the 1960s.)* (2.4 km).

4. Turn left, along the B4437 for 400 m, then take the 2nd road left, skirting **Cornbury Park** on your left. Continue up to the Church and "*The Bell*" PH and turn left, then left again at "*The Bull*" PH (tel. 01608 810689) to rejoin the B4437. Go downhill, over river and railway bridges.

5. After 700 m, take the farm track bridleway (GR.349195) to **Walcot Fm.**, on your right, then go due west across undulating fields, with splendid Evenlode valley views, to Catsham Lane (1.7 km).

6. Choose either :- 6A) or 6B)

6A) Dogleg right into **Shorthampton Fm**. road (0.6 km) and continue west then southwest across fields to **Chilson** (1 km). Go left, for 100 m of minor road, to a bridleway (a farm track then fields) on the right leading southwest to Yew Tree Farm, **Ascott d'Oyley** (1.5 km). Take the lane into **Ascott-u-Wychwood.** At a "T" junction ("*The Swan*" *PH is down to the right*), turn left up the hill. Cross the B4437 (CARE) at 800m. (GR307180) into a bridleway farm lane (verge) leading southeast through **Kingstanding Fm.** to Fiveash Bottom and **Hatching Hill**. Turn right on Hatching Lane (2.5 km).

6B). Turn left and cross the B4437 (CARE) (0.4km) onto a minor road (verges) going south, past **Ranger's Lawn** and bear right at **Ranger's Lodge**. The route on a rural road, in part goes through, and in part skirts, **Wychwood Forest** (*The present 600 acre Cornbury Park, is a modest residue from a vast Saxon Royal deerforest. The medieval hunting lodge, given by Queen Elizabeth I to the Earl of Leicester, was replaced by a 17 C. Restoration mansion designed by Nicholas Stone, mason-sculptor to Inigo Jones, for Edward Hyde, 1st Earl of Clarendon, who was Charles II's Lord Chancellor until he criticised the latter's immorality).*

7. Continue south by road (*"Hatching Lane*") into **Lower End**, **Leafield.** *(The travellor Arthur Young in 1813 said:"The area is filled with poachers, deer stealers, thieves and pilferers of every kind .....Oxford gaol would be uninhabited were it not for this fertile source of crimes").* Turn left at the "T" junction for 400 m to the farm lane on your right immediately after a PH (GR.326155). Fork left at 400 m along a green lane BOAT ("*Pay Lane*") now rather degraded and overgrown, going southeast for 1.7 km.

Cross (CARE) over the B4022 and a minor road junction at New Found Out Farm, (GR.343145). *(Take the minor road second left, along roman "Akeman Street", to reach "The Royal Oak" PH,* ***Ramsden*** *tel. 01993 868213*). The green lane opposite (a BOAT, "*St. John's Lane*") leads to a "T" road junction (1.4 km). Continue southeast along the minor road opposite, past **Gigley Farm** & Nursery, for 700 m to a minor road (Delly End to Northleigh). Turn left to return to the Start.

THE DANDY.

30 "John Cottington, *alias* Mull Sack, robbing the Oxford Wagon."

Route 8:-CHARLBURY and WYCHWOOD FOREST

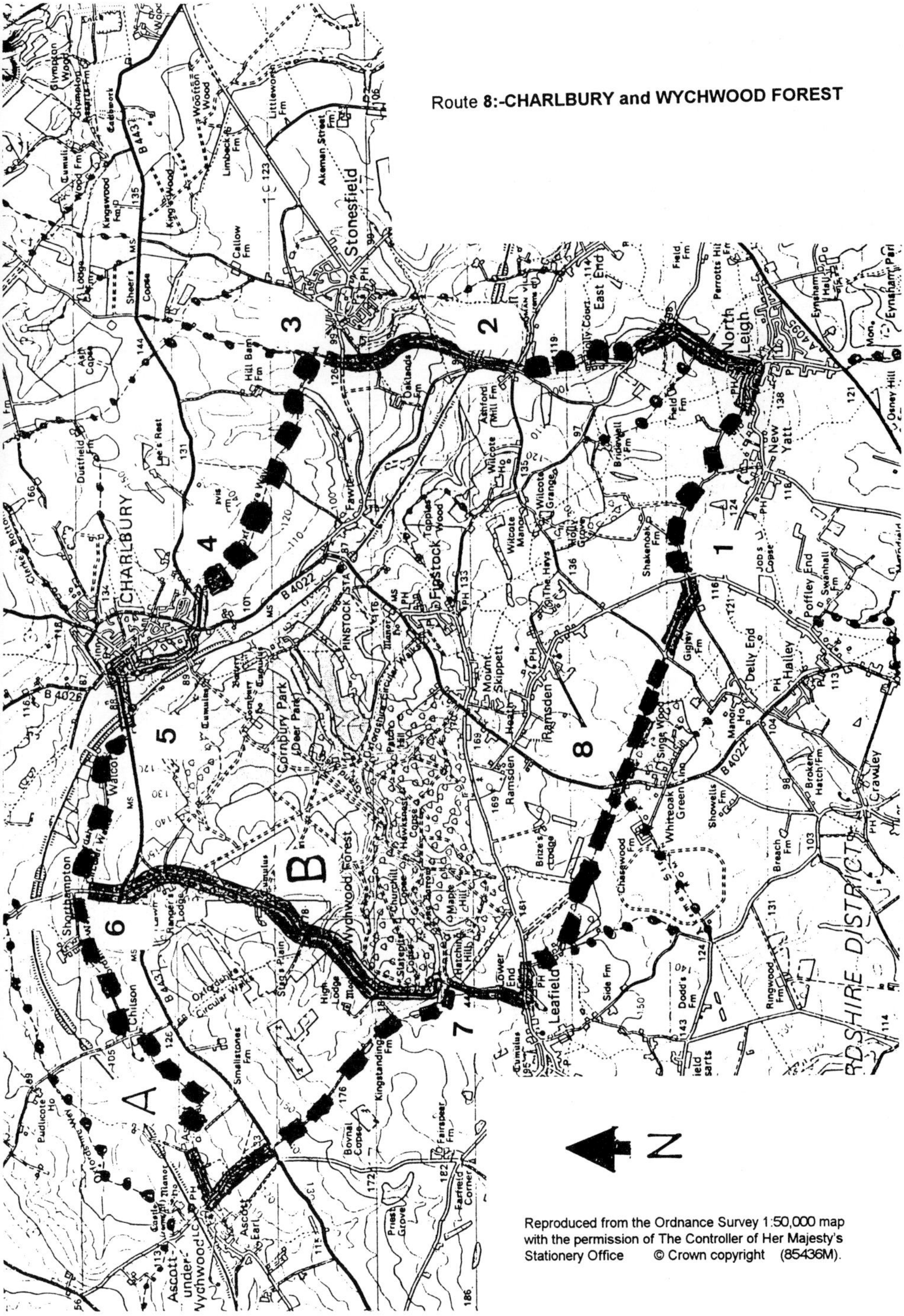

Reproduced from the Ordnance Survey 1:50,000 map with the permission of The Controller of Her Majesty's Stationery Office © Crown copyright (85436M).

ASCOTT u WYCHWOOD & the lower EVENLODE VALLEY
Route 9

14 miles, circular (clockwise)
Ordnance Survey maps:
Landranger 163,164,
Pathfinder 1068, 1091
Length:
14 miles (23 km) in total, of which
9 miles (14 km). bridleway.
Starting and Parking point:-
Crown Farm, Ascott u Wychwood,
(plse. tel. 01993 830307), (GR.301186)

Route description

Start. From **Ascott-u-Wychwood** cross the railway and river to the field bridleway on your left which rises across 4 fields (1.1km). Cross the A361 (CARE) into the minor road opposite and go down to **Lynham** (1.1km).

1. Turn right onto a bridleway track (Point 1) which goes due east then northeast on rising ground (1.8 km) to a hedge boundary just before the A361 *(by the Lyneham Barrow and Settlement sites at* GR.295212) and some 200 m alt.

2. Turn left onto a field bridleway (Point 9) going north along a right-hand hedge and then across two fields and a farm track above **Merriscourt Fm.** *(Lord Moreton erected twin pillars and a stone seat here at his favourite bellevedere*). Continue north to **Fairgreen Fm.** and a green lane bridleway down to Sarsden lake (GR.293227).

3. Continue up towards **Sarsden House** (Point 10) *(a late 17 C mansion now being restored in a park landscaped by Humphrey Repton)* (2km). Turn right at Home Farm onto a road with a medieval cross and ride northeast (verge) to a minor road (Churchill to Chadlington). Cross over into the "no through road" opposite which becomes a track bridleway through **Sarsgrove Woods** to the A361 (2.5 km). Exit left (CARE) for 150 m. (verge) and at road junction in the dip (CARE because of the A361 bend), cross right into the minor road (verge) going southeast up to a caravan camp then down Barley Hill into **Chadlington** (mapped as alternative A).

4. After a children's playground at **Millend** (Point 12), take the first road left, then at the bowling club turn right towards the church and then left again. At **Eastend**, take a field bridleway northeast to the paddock of **Dean** Manor (700 m). Turn right onto the road and take the field bridleway opposite going south-east down to a brook and spinney. Turn right and continue by road to **Spelsbury** (1 km).

5. Turn right at the four alms-houses *(built in 1689 by Jon Carey, the Ditchley estate agent)* (Point 13) and follow the lane behind the farm, south east along a track to a field bridleway on your right going southwest to **Coldron Brook**. Detour to the right round the edge of a former quarry, now a waste disposal site. Turn left into Grove Lane and then turn right onto field bridleway which goes down to a brook and then up to Greenhill Copse. Continue on a field edge bridleway.

6. Cross Catsham Lane (Point 14) on a field bridleway going west along the Evenlode valley only one field away from the river.

7. Cross Pudlicote Lane (Point 15) (1.7km) and then continue southwest following the River Evenlode upstream. This bridleway is part of the "Oxfordshire Way" and finishes on the river bank and the bridge over the river at **Ascott-u-Wychwood** *(Manor, site of medieval castle)* (2 km).

8. Alternative E (from Point 9) Continue to the wooded *Settlement* and cross the A361

(CARE) into Pudlicote Lane opposite. Go southeast past **Pudlicote Ho.** to the field bridleway near the River Evenlode bridge (Point 15) & return.

9. Alternative D (from Point 9). Continue to the wooded *Settlement* at the A361 and cross (CARE) into Pudlicote Lane opposite. After 100 m, turn left along the road past **Barter's Hill Fm**. (good verges) down to **Greenend, Brookend, Westend** and then **Eastend** of **Chadlington** (Point 12).

10. Alternative C (from Point 10). At **Sarsden** Lake, take a bridleway on the right, rising up through woods eastwards but then turn southeast out of the spinney into a field bridleway climbing sharply up to a small wood. Bear right, cross over the farm road to **Fairgreen Fm.** into a cross-field bridleway leading to a "T" road-junction at the A361. Cross (CARE) into Cross's Lane opposite and ride downhill (verges) to **Brookend** and turn left to **Westend & Eastend.** (Point 12).

11. Alternative B (from Point 10). At **Sarsden** Lake, take a bridleway on the right, rising up through woods east then northeast, joining a new estate roadway and exit at a road fork. Take the lefthand fork (verge) to the impressive semi-circular estate walls at the "T" road-junction on the A361. Cross (CARE) into the minor road opposite and ride down to **Millend.** You pass *"The Tite" PH* with good parking. (*"Tite" is O.E. for 'spring'*). At a children's playing field, turn right for 200 m then left and right to the Church at Chadlington (Point 12).

12. From **Sarsden Ho**. Home Farm (Point 11) you can turn right, past the old cross, then turn right again on a tree lined verge due east to the road fork mentioned in "B" para. 11 above.[1]

BRUERN ABBEY & the upper EVENLODE VALLEY

Route 10

14 miles, figure-of-eight
Ordnance Survey maps:
Landranger 163,164,
Pathfinder 1068, 1091
Length:
14 miles (23 km) in total, of which
10 miles (16 km) bridleway.
Starting and parking points:-
i) Crown Farm Ascott u Wychwood, (plse. tel. .01993 830307) (GR.301186)
ii) Pebbly Hill Stud, Bledington (tel 01608 659743) (GR.233230) (Point 4).

Route description

Start. From **Ascott-u-Wychwood** cross the railway and river to the field bridleway on your left which rises across 4 fields (1.1km.). Cross the A361 (CARE) into the minor road opposite and go down to **Lynham** (1.1 km).

1. Turn left, west along the minor road past Priory Farm riding under the railway towards **Heath Farm** (1.8 km).

2. Turn right on a bridleway leading to woods and **Bruern Abbey** (1.4 km) (Point 3). *(The abbey has been in turn, a 12C Cistercian abbey, an 18C mansion and now a school).*

3. Turn left along the road to Milton under Wychwood and choose 3(A) or 3(B).

3(A) After 500 m, where the road bends south, take the cross-field bridleway going northwest, then southwest, to Snowhill Plantation.

3(B) After 300 m, turn right into a farm road running along the side of Cocksmoor Copse north west to **Foxholes**. A field-edge bridleway on the left leads from **Fifield Heath** south west and round to the east side of **Herbert's Heath.** Turn west along the south edge of **Herbert's Heath** and climb up across five fields to **Idbury** (170 m alt.) (2.4 km). At the road, turn left, then right at the church, to **Nether Westcote** (1 km). Turn right to *"The New Inn"* PH at the start of a green lane bridleway which drops down to **Pebbly Hill Stud** (Point 4) (3 km). Take the field bridleway opposite **Pebbly Hill Farm,** go across 4 fields to exit, right, onto the B4450. Go right for 200 m and turn left along the farm track bridleway northeast through **Bledington Grounds.** Ride northeast along the west side of **Bledington Heath** towards **Lower Oddington** (4 km). *(The only remains of a former village is the 13 C St. Nicholas' Church which contains a restored 14C. "Doom" wall painting, a 15 C font & Jacobean pulpit, all treasures endowed by various Kings & Archbishops. The village has moved uphill to* **Upper Oddington** *and "The Horse & Groom" PH.).*

4. Take the cross-field bridleway at the northwest corner of **Bledington Heath** (Point 5) and ride northeast down to bridges across the **River Evenlode** & the railway at **Daylesford** *(where Warren Hasting of the East India Company was born and buried).* Turn right and head southeast for 1 km to an isolated barn; where the field on your right has a bridleway back to the railway. (*The farm track goes straight ahead for 1 km to the shaded streets and village green at* ***Kingham*** *and "The Plough" PH. with a coaching yard*). Recross the railway and then the river, the latter on a narrow wooden bridge with gates at both ends. From the water meadows (*beloved by Warde Fowler, the Oxford ornithologist*) turn left, south, onto a farm track and then left onto the B4450 road towards Bledington village (1.5 km).

Route **9:-ASCOTT-u.-WYCHWOOD**

& the lower EVENLODE VALLEY

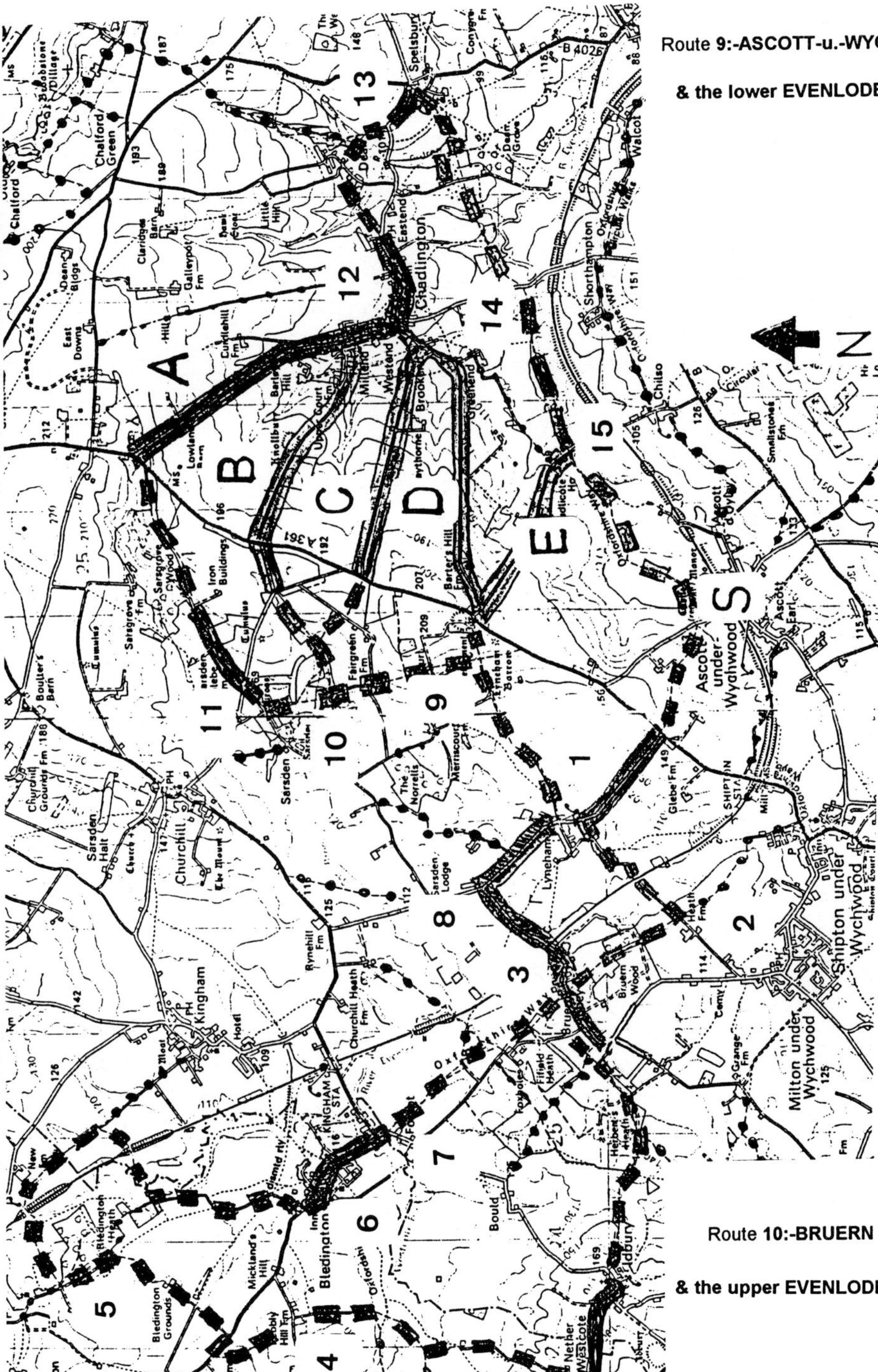

Route **10:-BRUERN ABBEY**

& the upper EVENLODE VALLEY

5. From **Bledington** *(a village green with ducks, a babbling brook and "The Kings' Head" PH)* (Point 6) continue south by road to a "T" road-junction (Kingham & Idbury). Fork right to **Foscot**.

6. After 150 m, (Point 7) at the bend before Foxcote Farm, enter on your left a bridleway which goes southeast across four fields to the woods by **Foxholes Fm.** Continue southeast on a wooded and often boggy bridleway past Cocksmore Copse to **Bruern Abbey** (2.2 km) (Point 3). Turn left along the road going east and pass **Bruern Abbey** on your right. Cross the Evenlode and railway going northeast to a "T" road-junction at Sarsden Gorse.

7. Turn right along the road and the front of the Golf Course for 1 km to **Lyneham** village (Point 1). Continue uphill to the "T" road-junction on the A361. Cross (CARE) into the cross-field bridleway opposite which returns down to the start at Ascott under Wychwood.

8. An extra minicircuit (7 km). From Westcote Brook, two fields south of **Pebbly Hill** Stud (Point 4) turn west on a field bridleway, recross the brook and follow a farm track on rising ground to **Gawcombe** House and farm buildings (both modern and traditional, including a stableyard with dovecot). Continue up the wooded drive and turn left along the minor road for 1 km to **Church Westcote**. Turn first left into a green lane bridleway (sometimes boggy), and rejoin the bridleway route from **Nether Westcote** two fields before Westcote Brook [1]

49 A well-loaded Stage-Wagon
From a drawing of ca. 1820 by J. L. Agasse

HOOK NORTON, Balscote & Traitors Ford Route 11

22 miles, circular (anti-clockwise)
Ordnance Survey maps:
Landranger 151,
Pathfinder 1044, 1045, 1021 & 1022
Length:
22 miles (34 km) in total, of which
13 miles (20 km) bridleway.
Several shorter alternatives.

Parking & starting point:

(i) O.C.C. layby, Wiggington Heath cross -roads, (GR.385352) west of Bloxham
(ii) "*Horse & Groom*" PH park Milcombe (Plse tel Mr. & Mrs. Roger Nicholls 01295 720471) (GR.408345)

Route description

1. Take a field bridleway 500 m west of **Milcombe,** going north across two undulating fields to twin hunting gates. Contour northeast across a third field to a "WH" (Warwickshire Hunt) gate. In field No 4, turn left riding up the bank to another "WH" gate by a copse. Drop down field No 5 to another hunt gate. Bear right along the hedge of field No 6 to a farm gate into the last field. Turn left to a track into the dairycow collecting yards of **Lower Tadmarton Fm**. (2.5 km).

2. At the farm entrance, turn left along B4035 for 200 m (CARE), then turn right into Shutford Road for 50 m, then immediately turn again right along a lane for 100 m, to a field bridleway up a steep bank on your left. Go diagonally right to a badly hung field gate leading north east through a plantation of young trees.

3. Choose 3 (A) or 3 (B).

3 (A) The public bridleway route continues ahead, north east, along one hedge before turning due north as a cross-field path to a hunting gate into **Fulling Mill Fm**.

3 (B) A permissive bridleway was created here in 1995 (which the landowner, Broughton Estates, has provided and "*hopes will be used instead of the existing public route*"). After the trees, turn left, north, along a wide field edge path, then turn right, east, to a stone barn. Turn left along a hard track west to a metal barn and then turn right along a field edge path to join an unmetalled county road. Turn right down to a gate into **Fulling Mill Fm**.

4. Continue due north, uphill past Fulling Mill Fm to a fork in the road. Turn sharp left along the farm track past **Broughton Grounds Fm.** to a barn on the Shutford to North Newington road. Turn right along the road for 250 m.

5. Turn left into a field edge bridleway which rises steeply up **Claydon Hill.** Enter a hunting gate into the covert and go along its east side. Turn left along its northern edge. Cross two fields going west and drop down to Wroxton Mill (*now a private house with its own golf course).* Dog-leg 50 m right along the minor road to a field bridleway (GR.398405). Go north west, then due north, left of a reservoir to a gate and track to Priory Farm, **Balscote** (3 km).

6. Take the road left; turn right at the PH and then left again at the lovely Church in warm Cotswold stone (*Decorated style and a tower over its south porch*) to a "T" road-junction (1.2 km). Take the field bridleway opposite down to a brook. *(On your right a bridleway contours northeast for 1.5 km, up to* ***Shenington*** *and "The Bell" PH tel.01295 670274*). Cross left, southwest up a steep field, continuing southwest past a barn towards, but turning right just before, **Epwell Grounds Fm.** Go across one field,

over a green lane and two more fields to a "T" road-junction.(2 km).

7. Take the road opposite (verge) into **Epwell** ("*The Chandler's Arms*" PH. tel.01295 780344) and bear left through the village to a "T" road-junction at Heath Plantation (2 km).

8. Take the field bridleway opposite, by **Sibford Heath Fm** (brand new gates) south west across two fields to B4035. Turn right (part verge) for 300 m. At the Warwicks county boundary, cross over (CARE) to a green lane bridleway ("*Ditchedge Lane*") going south near **Gallow Hill Fm.** (CARE rabbit holes !).

9. (A detour) After 1 km you can make a 1.3 km detour left south east down a green lane to a stream. Enter and then climb up a banky field to Manor Farm, **Sibford Gower**. Turn right (*past "The Wykham Arms"PH tel.01295 780351 with shaded grazing).* Continue by road south for 800 m passing **The Colony** cottages down to two opposing field gates. Turn right, west, and climb on a 800 m. bridleway track back up to "*Ditchedge Lane*".

10. The green lane, on a ridge forming the Warwickshire border, becomes a field edge bridleway as it drops down two steep fields to the road at **Traitor's Ford** (2.8 km).

11. Continue south-southwest by road along Traitor's Ford Lane (verges) past the prominent radiomast and road-junction on **Wichford Hill** (239 m alt).

12. At Wychford Lodge Farm, (3.5 km) (GR.328333) take the bridleway farmtrack left, going due south past **Court Fm**. and then curving southeast, in a green lane then across fields, to join the **Hook Norton** road at a bend (2.5 km).

13. At the "T" road-junction, where the Hook road goes north, continue ahead due east on the Swerford road (verges) for 1.5 km. Turn right, south, down a tree-lined bridleway drive to **Swerford Park**, then turn left at the House onto a field bridleway (*a permissive route; instead of the public bridleway which goes through the gardens in front of the house*) leading east to a minor road above Broadstones Stud (1.8 km). Take the bridleway track opposite, going down to a glade and continue east past Cradle Barn to join a minor lane (1 km). (Alternatively turn right for 200 m *to see the fine workmanship of the artistic wrought iron gates* and take the same lane in the valley to your left).

14. Follow this lane (verges) northeast to **Wiggington** and then north back to Wiggington Heath cross-roads (3.5 km).

15. Turn right to return to **Milcombe** by road (CARE no verge).

16. Additional routes

At least ten bridleways within, and several outside, this "great circle" route offer many possible variations, including the Warwickshire escarpment near **Edgehill**. But it may be useful to remember that this undulating Cotswold countryside, with many stock rearing farms, small fields and numerous gates, needs time to enjoy.[1]

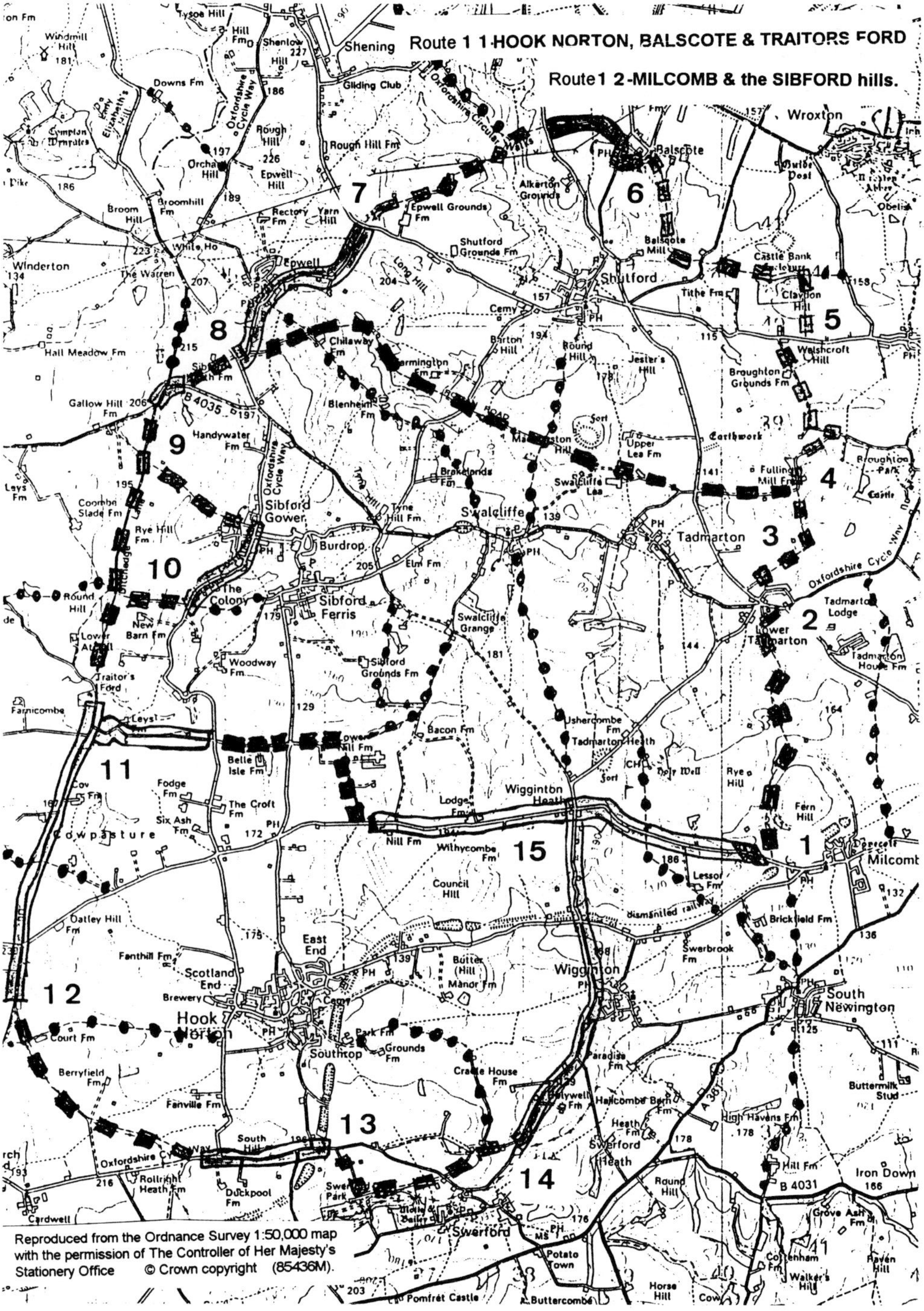
Route 1 1-HOOK NORTON, BALSCOTE & TRAITORS FORD
Route1 2-MILCOMB & the SIBFORD hills.
Reproduced from the Ordnance Survey 1:50,000 map with the permission of The Controller of Her Majesty's Stationery Office © Crown copyright (85436M).
Shenington
Gliding Club
Oxfordshire Circular Walks
Oxfordshire Cycle Way
Tysoe Hill
Windmill Hill
Downs Fm
Shenlow Hill
Rough Hill
Rough Hill Fm
Orchard Hill
Epwell Hill
Broom Hill
Broomhill Fm
Rectory Fm
Yarn Hill
Epwell Grounds Fm
Epwell
Winderton
The Warren
White Ho
Alkerton Grounds
Balscote
Balscote Mill
Wroxton
Shutford Grounds Fm
Shutford
Long Hill
Tithe Fm
Castle Bank
Claydon Hill
Cemy
Barton Hill
Round Hill
Jester's Hill
Welshcroft Hill
Broughton Grounds Fm
Hall Meadow Fm
Chilaway Fm
Farmington Fm
Blenheim Fm
Gallow Hill Fm
B 4035
Handywater Fm
Madmarston Hill
Fort
Upper Lea Fm
Earthwork
Swalcliffe Lea
Fulling Mill Fm
Broughton Park
Brakelands Fm
Tyne Hill
Tyne Hill Fm
Swalcliffe
Tadmarton
Leys Fm
Coombe Slade Fm
Sibford Gower
Rye Hill Fm
Burdrop
Elm Fm
Round Hill
The Colony
Sibford Ferris
Swalcliffe Grange
Tadmarton Lodge
Lower Tadmarton
New Barn Fm
Lower Atchill
Traitor's Ford
Woodway Fm
Sibford Grounds Fm
Tadmarton House Fm
Farnicombe
Leys
Bacon Fm
Ushercombe Fm
Tadmarton Heath
Belle Isle Fm
Lower Nill Fm
Holy Well
Rye Hill
Fodge Fm
The Croft Fm
Six Ash Fm
Cowpasture
Lodge Fm
Wigginton Heath
Fern Hill
Nill Fm
Withycombe Fm
Milcomb
Lessor Fm
Council Hill
Dismantled railway
Brickfield Fm
Oatley Hill Fm
East End
Fanthill Fm
Scotland End
Brewery
Butter Hill
Manor Fm
Wigginton
Swerbrook Fm
South Newington
Hook Norton
Court Fm
Southrop
Park Fm
Grounds Fm
Cradle House Fm
Paradise Fm
Berryfield Fm
Fanville Fm
Hollywell Fm
Hallcombe Barn Fm
Heath Fm
Swerford Heath
Buttermilk Stud
High Havens Fm
South Hill
Oxfordshire Cycle Way
Rollright Heath Fm
Duckpool Fm
Swerford Park
Motte & Bailey
Swerford
Round Hill
Hill Fm
B 4031
Iron Down
Grove Ash Fm
Cardwell
Potato Town
Cottenham Fm
Walker's Hill
Raven Hill
Pomfret Castle
Buttercombe
Horse Hill
1 2 3 4 5 6 7 8 9 10 11 12 13 14 15

14 miles, circular (anti-clockwise)
Ordnance Survey maps:
Landranger 151,
Pathfinder 1044, 1045, 1021 & 1022
Length:
14 miles (22 km) in total, of which
10 miles (16 km) bridleway.
A shorter winter alternative (linking Points 1, 4, 8, 11 and 15) to Route 11.

Parking & starting point:

(i) O.C.C. layby, Wiggington Heath cross-roads (GR.385352) west of Bloxham
(ii) "*Horse & Groom*" PH park Milcombe (Plse tel. Mr. & Mrs. Roger Nicholls 01295 720471) (GR.408345)

Route description

1. Take a field bridleway 500 m west of **Milcombe**, (Point 1) going north across two undulating fields to twin hunting gates. Contour northeast across a third field to a "WH" (Warwickshire Hunt) gate. In field No 4, turn left riding up the bank to another "WH" gate by a copse. Drop down field No 5 to another hunt gate. Bear right along the hedge of field No 6 to a farm gate into the last field. Turn left to a track into the dairycow collecting yards of **Lower Tadmarton Fm**. (2.5 km).

2. At the farm entrance, (Point 2) turn left along B4035 for 200 m (CARE), then turn right into Shutford Road for 50 m then immediately turn again right along a lane for 100 m, to a field bridleway up a steep bank on your left. Go diagonally right to a badly hung field gate leading northeast through a plantation of young trees.

3. Choose 3 (A) or 3 (B).
3 (A) The public bridleway route continues ahead, northeast, along one hedge before turning due north as a cross-field path to a hunting gate into **Fulling Mill Fm**.
3 (B) A permissive bridleway was created here in 1995 (which the landowner, Broughton Estates, has provided and "*hopes will be used instead of the existing public route*"). After the trees, turn left, north, along a wide field-edge path, then right, east, to a stone barn. First turn left on a hard track to a metal barn, then right on a field-edge path to join an unmetalled county road leading to **Fulling Mill Fm**.

4. Turn left, due west, and drop down to the Shutford to Lower Tadmarton Road. Cross into the minor road opposite After 300 m, fork right onto the road past **Swalcliffe Lea** and continue north west. below **Madmarston Hill Fort** for 3 km onto a hard track (*a former Roman road*). Cross the minor road coming from Shutford into the field edge bridleway opposite, which becomes a green lane near **Farmington Fm**. before it bends right and drops down to a field edge path passing a large duck pond. Follow left-hand hedges to a drunken field gate and ford the stream (footbridge and *kingfishers* here). Bear left, due west, along the left hedge on rising ground up to **Chilaway Fm.**

5. Choose 5 (A) or 5 (B).
5 (A).Take the field bridleway on the right to the village green at **Epwell.** Turn left to "*The Chandler's Arms*" PH. tel.01295 780344. Bear left through the village to Heath Plantation.
5 (B). Take the Chilaway Fm driveway going south west to the road at Heath Plantation (Point 8).

6. At the "T" junction by **Heath Plantation**, (Point 8) take the field

bridleway opposite, by **Sibford Heath Fm** south west across two fields (new gates) to B4035. Turn right for 500 m (part verge) to the Warwicks county boundary, cross over (CARE) to a green lane bridleway ("*Ditchedge Lane*") near **Gallow Hill Fm**. going south (rabbit holes).

7. (A detour) After 1 km (Point 9) you can make a 1.3 km detour left south east down a green lane to a stream. Enter and then climb up a banky field to Manor Farm, **Sibford Gower**. Turn right ("*The Wykham Arms" PH tel. 01295 780351)* and continue by road south for 800m passing **The Colony** cottages down to two gates into opposing bridleways. Turn right, west, climbing on a 800 m track back up to "*Ditchedge Lane*".

8. The green lane bridleway, (Point 10) on a ridge forming the Warwickshire border, becomes a field edge bridleway as it drops down two steep fields (with rabbit holes!) to the road at **Traitor's Ford** (2.8 km).

9. Continue south by road and turn left (Point 11) past **Leys Fm**. to the Sibford Gower to Hook Norton road. Cross over into the farm track bridleway opposite and continue due east below **Belle Isle Fm** to the Sibford Ferris to Hook Norton road. Cross into the bridleway track opposite as far as the cluster of farm buildings at **Lower Nill Fm.** Turn right onto the farm service road and continue slightly uphill to the road at Nill Cottages. Turn left and return along the road (verges) past **Lodge Fm** and Turpins Lodge Riding School to Wiggington Heath cross roads. Continue ahead by road (CARE no verge) to **Milcombe**.[1]

40 Travellers taking refreshment at a Country Alehouse, while a Stage-Wagon rumbles by

From a print of ca. 1800

Route 13:-CROPREDY and the CHERWELL VALLEY

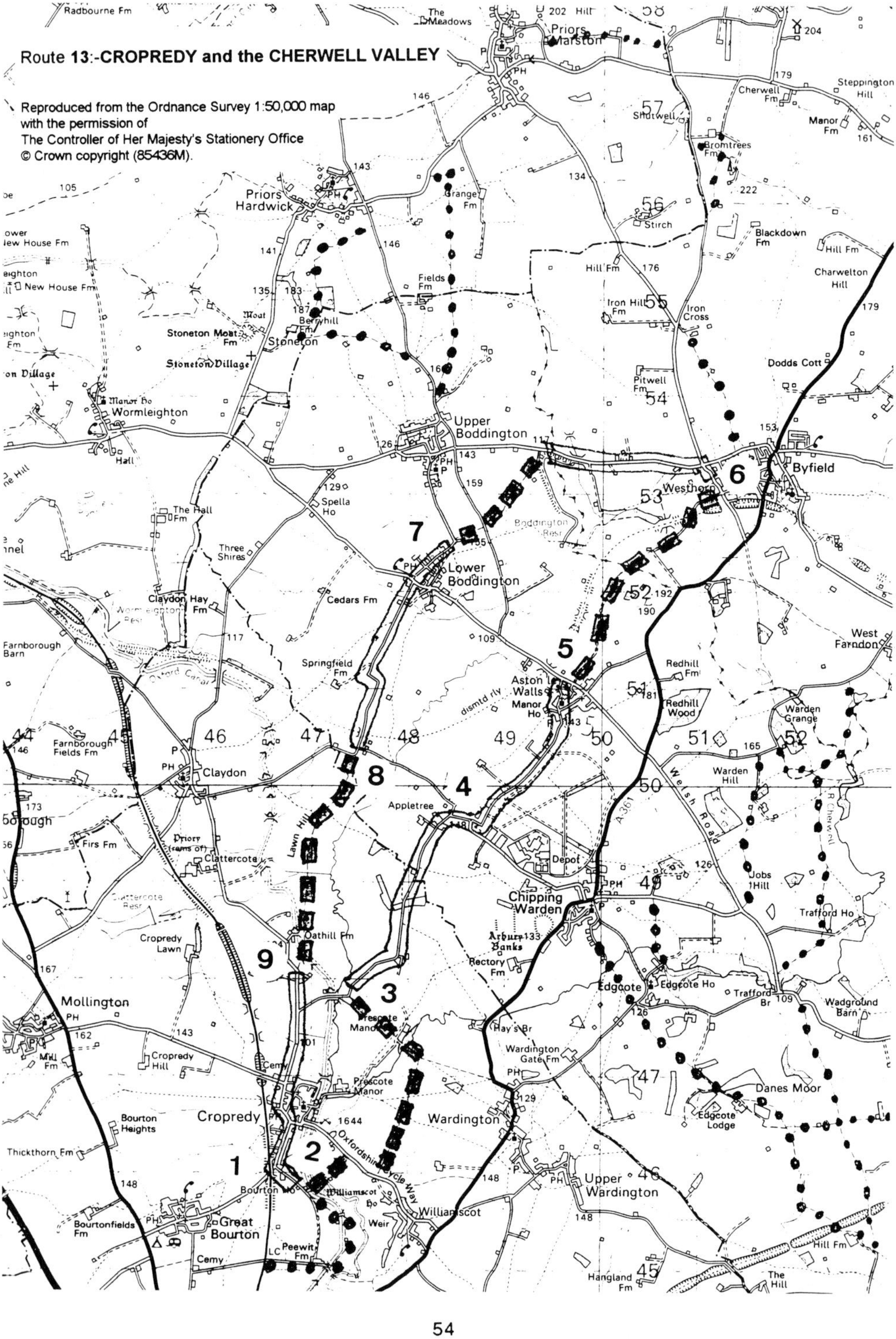

14 miles, circular (anti-clockwise)
Ordnance Survey maps:
Landranger 151,
Pathfinder 999, 1022
Length:
14 miles (22 km) in total, of which
6 miles (10 km) bridleway.
Parking & starting points:
a) Verge between Gt.Bourton & Cropredy, (GR.464458) 1 mile east of A423(T)
(ii) Boddington Resr. (GR.495533) 1.5 mile west of Byfield, A361.

Route description

1. Take the road (verge) from **Great Bourton** (*where "The Bell" PH stands opposite a 14 C church with a combined lychgate and belfry in Cotswold stone*) to **Cropredy.** Go under the railway bridge and turn first right, passing the school on your left and **Bourton Ho**. on your right to the brick watermill and stables at the end of Mill Lane. [A diversion: an extra 3 km out & return. *This pleasant, all-bridleway addition is a rare example in Oxfordshire of a public bridleway along a canal towpath, previously used by barge horses.* Take the field bridleway at the entrance to **Peewit Fm**. and go diagonally left to a bridge over the canal. Turn right on the towpath south to the next bridge. Cross the canal, pass **Peewit Fm** and continue due West to the British Railway pedestrians-only level crossing. This is the point of obligatory return. [*Although this same "Mill Lane" bridleway continues due west to the Bourton road and is 30 ft wide under an Enclosure Act, the **L.C.** level crossing was downgraded in 1980 to a footpath*].

2. At the brick watermill, turn east over the canal bridge to a field bridleway going north east to the **Williamscot** road. Turn right for 350 m. Enter the field bridleway opposite Lower Lodge by the upper of two gateways and go northeast on falling ground. *(To the left, is the site of the 1644 Civil War battle for this strategic river bridge, with about 5000 cavalry and 4000 infantry on each side. The King defeated General Sir William.Waller MP. who was the first to suggest creating a "New Model" professional army. Waller, a moderate Presbyterian not a Puritan, was later imprisoned for opposing Cromwell's Commonwealth).* Turn northwest to cross, first, the River Cherwell, then a farm track to Prescote Manor Farm. Follow the bridleway across two fields to a minor road (2.4 km).

3. Turn right along the road for 2 km on rising ground past **Appletree Ho**. **& Fm** to a "T" road-junction. (*Traces of a medieval village can be seen from the other side of the valley near Point 8*).

4. Turn right towards Chipping Warden, but keep straight ahead at the next "T" junction, going north on a minor road to **Aston le Walls** (2 km). Fork left to a "T" junction. Turn right for 50 m (verge). and cross into the bridleway opposite.

5. From the telegraph pole, follow the righthand hedge down and then up to a green lane which contours left, and goes north, then northeast, to a derelict field barn. Dogleg right, down to a disused railway bridge and a bridleway track into **Westhorp** and **Byfield** (2.7 km).

6. At "*The Twistle*" (*a road, not a PH*) turn left and left again at the crossroads, following the road down past **Boddington Reservoir**. Take the field bridleway on the

left which rises south west, across a minor road, to **Lower Boddington.**

7. Turn left and at the cross roads (by the PH) continue south taking the minor road opposite towards **Claydon** and a minor "T" road-junction from Chipping Warden.

8. Where the road bends right, continue ahead on a cross-field bridleway which contours as a field-edge bridleway southwest down to a narrow field under **Lawn Hill**. Continue due south, across flat fields. Near **Oathill Fm** cross the canal bridge and exit onto the road.

9. Turn left along the road (verge) and return to **Cropredy.** (*The village, recorded under the Bishop of Lincoln in Doomsday Book, passed in 1547 to King Edward VI and was later sold by Queen Elizabeth I. "The Brasenose" PH. on the green indicates the Oxford college which bought the manor in 1788. Houses were built of Cotswold stone and thatch until the Oxford to Coventry Canal opened in 1790 and the Great Western Railway line in 1850, introducing cheap transport for red bricks and Welsh slate. The canal now provides popular cruising holidays. The Church of St. Mary the Virgin, part 11 C & part 14 C, has a 13 C oak chest, a brass lectern, and a lantern turret superimposed on the square tower to guide night-time travellers.*)

Alternative/additional routes

A. At the cross roads (Point 6), turn right for 300 m. Take the field bridleway north to **Iron Cross Fm.** Take the right fork along the minor road towards **Hellidon** and go over the the cross roads, taking a field bridleway left at the bend, due west to **Priors Marston**. Turn left (or right) going down into and through the village. Follow the road south & then southwest towards **Priors Hardwick**. A field bridleway on the left after **Grange Fm.** leads due south to **Upper Boddington** (alt.168 m). Go by road (verge) to **Lower Boddington** (Point 7).

B. From **Appletree** (Point 4), follow the road past the Lynx Car depot on a former airfield to **Chipping Warden** (1.5 km). Cross the A361 (CARE) diagonally left to the church & cross. Fork left into a *cul de sac* leading to a green lane with a small but splendid stone bridge over the infant River Cherwell. Take the bridleway up to **Edgcote** (NB *harmonious architecture of mansion, family church, stables set in parkland with thoroughbred horses).* At the road-junction take the cross-field bridleway opposite southeast to join a metalled estate road rising up to **Edgcote Lodge.** Turn east, down the left side of the Old Spinney, and then go southeast cross-field to a corner of **Danes Moor**. Go through the ditch and follow the left hedgerow heading east towards **Culworth**. After a field barn, where two bridleways cross in the valley, turn left onto a track going north. Where the track bends right to buildings, take a field edge bridleway to a hunting gate. At the road, turn left then right over **Trafford Bridge,** and go north to the "T" road-junction below **Jobs Hill**. Turn left and turn left again opposite "Calves Close", onto a farm track bridleway down to Home Fm and the House at **Edgcote**.

C. Alternative B can be extended at **Trafford Bridge** by taking a cross-field bridleway northeast towards Trafford Ho. farm, but turning due north, up the hill and down into fields close to the **Cherwell**. Turn left, uphill to the wood and road above. Turn left along the road to **Warden Hill** and go due south by farmtrack and field bridleway to **Jobs Hill** and down to the "T" road-junction below.[1]

CHADLINGTON, DITCHLEY & WYCHWOOD Route 14

Two circular drives (clockwise).
Ordnance Survey maps:
Landranger 164,
Pathfinder 1068, 1069, 1091
Length (long & short drives):
Long : 19 miles (31 km) in total, of which
8 miles (13 km) BOAT.
Short: 14 miles (22 km) in total, of which
7 miles (11 km) BOAT.
Parking & starting point.
Bowling Club, Church Lane, Chadlington, (GR.332223) 3 miles southwest of Enstone.
Note of interest.
The Cherwell and West Oxfordshire Districts have few BOATs for carriage driving and the BOAT between Stonesfield and Chipping Norton is well worth a visit. It is 9 miles long and offers a direct (NW/SE) route along an attractive high Cotswolds ridge (up to 200 m alt.), on an all-weather, generally free-draining ground surface.
The route pays a small tribute to Sir Henry Rawlinson, born in Chadlington manor in 1810, who as an officer reorganizing the army of the Shah, transcribed from a rope over two years the trilingual cuneiform inscription of Darius I the Great on a 1700 foot cliff at Bisitun, Iran. He deciphered the Old Persian portion, published a translation with grammar & notes and with others had deciphered the Mesopotamian script by 1857, opening the way to much biblical, Babylonian, and Assyrian history. His locally trained horse "Coronation" won the Derby in 1841.

Route description

1. Go north for 1.5 miles along "Green Lane", a track which climbs gently up hill and passes near **Galleypot Fm**. At the Churchill to Lidstone road, turn right along the road for 3 miles passing **East Downs** farm buildings, the Chipping Norton road junction and the **Chalford Green** layby (opposite a "T" road-junction down to **Dean**). Then fork right on the road down to Spelsbury and Charlbury.

2. Where the road dips and turns sharply due south, continue ahead, along a green lane BOAT which goes southeast for 4.5 miles to Stonesfield. You cross first the minor Enstone to Spelsbury road and then the B4022 (Enstone to Charlbury) (CARE).

3. At **Shilcott Wood**, the green lane is joined from the right by a farm track (to **Norman's Grove)** on which the route continues to Hundley Way (a track down **Clarke's Bottom** to Charlbury) on the right and to the Charlbury Lodge entrance to **Ditchley Park** on the left (4 km). *(The Park has a **Model fm**. and some good examples of the Grim's Ditch, an Iron Age defensive system possibly between neighbouring tribes).* At **Dustfield Fm.**, the BOAT track becomes again a green lane and passes through an attractive picnic glade (GR.385195). Cross the B4437 (Charlbury to Oxford road) (CARE) into a fieldedge path which passes **Sheer's Copse** at Newbarn Fm. before turning south to the road at **Callow Fm**.

4. Turn right along the road into **Stonesfield**. At "*The White Horse*" PH (tel.01993 891604), take the right fork and bear right downhill to a bridleway on your right. Take the left fork past cottages and Spratt's Fm. garage then turn left, south, on the road to North Leigh crossing *Akeman Street* at the Common. After the railway bridge, the road drops to **Ashford Mill Fm.** on the River Evenlode. Turn

right, west, uphill and go straight over the first crossroads, passing **Wilcote Manor** and then **Wilcote Grange**. At a second, tangential, crossroads (Witney to Ramsden & the *"Royal Oak"* PH tel.01993 868213) continue southwest across to a "T" road-junction near **Gigley Fm.** and nursery (GR.357140).

5. Turn right into a green lane BOAT which runs in a straight line, west north-west, for 3 miles to Leafield, divided in two by the B4022 (Charlbury to Witney road). The first half (*"Saint John's Lane"*) by **St. John's** or **Singe Wood** leads down to the "T" junction at New Found Out Farm where a minor road from Ramsden joins the B4022. Continue across (CARE) into the second half opposite (*"Pay Lane"*) to Greenwich Lodge, Lower End, **Leafield**. (*These lanes, made boggy by arboreal overgrowth, could form a short, attractive figure-of-eight circuit if combined with "Riding Lane", an Inclosure award path 25 feet wide, running south from Greenwich Lodge to the Witney/Leafield road, with "Akeman Street" running from the Witney/Leafield road near Dodd's Plain northeast to New Found Out Fm. and with "Wood Lane",* ***Delly End****).*

6. At the Lower End PH, turn left along the road into **Leafield** and then right into Hatching Lane. To the left is *"The Fox" PH. tel. 01993 87647,* the village green, and the tall spire of a Victorian church (*built in 1859 by Sir George Gilbert Scott, later architect of the Albert Memorial, St. Pancras Station and other Gothic revivals*). Go due north for 5 miles via **Wychwood Forest**, fork left at **Ranger's Lodge** and cross the B4437 (CARE) into Catsham Lane. Cross two bridleways in the Evenlode valley to return to **Chadlington**.

A short alternative.(14 miles)

Turn round either at **Stonesfield** village or at the picnic area by **Dustfield Fm**.(see para.3 above). and return along the BOAT. At the fork by **Shilcott Wood**, north of **Norman's Grove**, bear left to go west. Cross the B4022 Enstone to Charlbury road (CARE) onto a minor road down to Lower Farm then up to the village cross at **Taston** (Point 7) (2 miles). Turn left along the road to **Spelsbury** (1 mile). Take the second road on the right and return to **Chadlington** (2 miles). The road right, after the Church, leads back to the Start.[1]

A SORRY CONVEYANCE.

MILITARY TURNOUT.

Route 14:-CHADLINGTON, DITCHLEY & WYCHWOOD

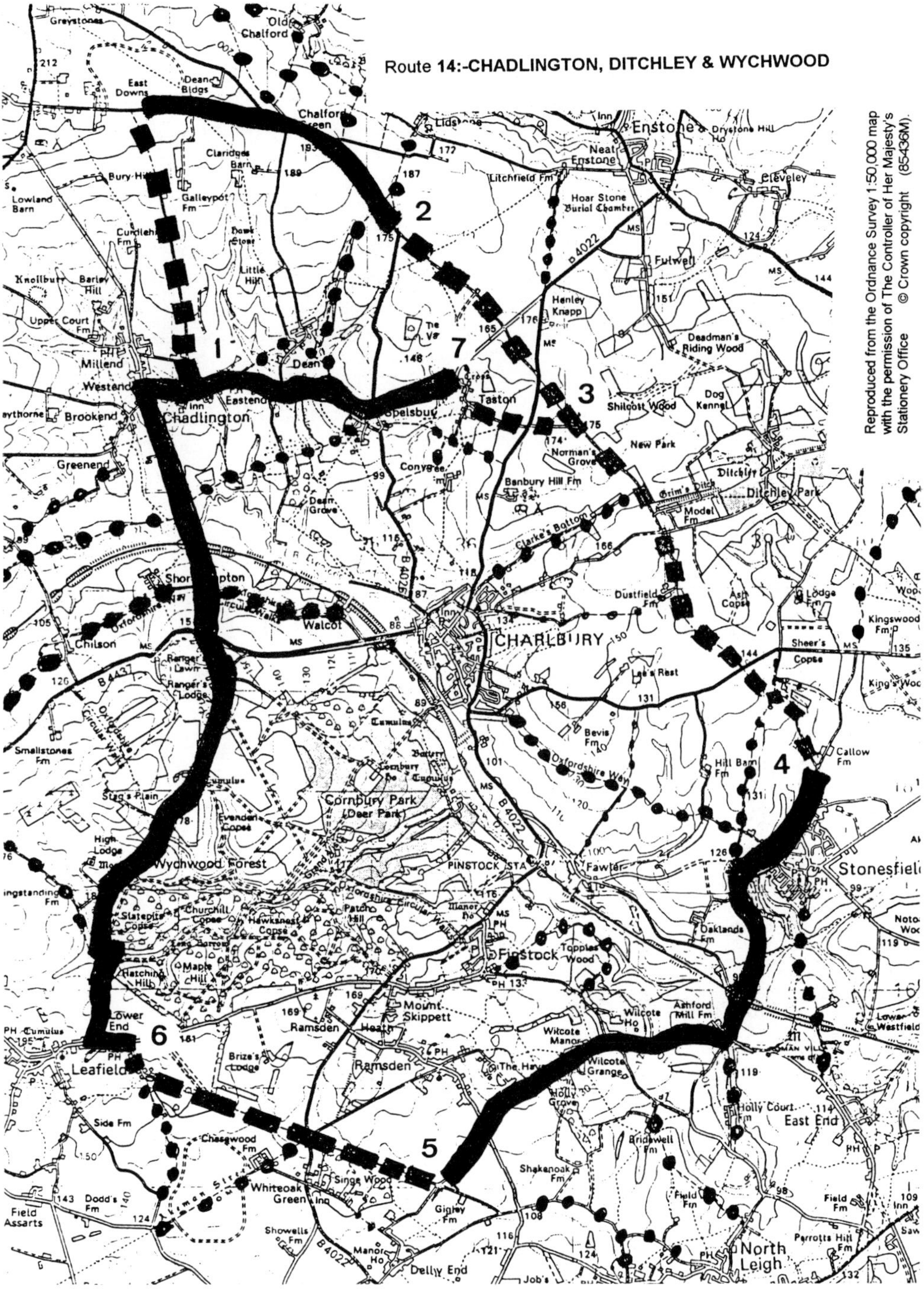

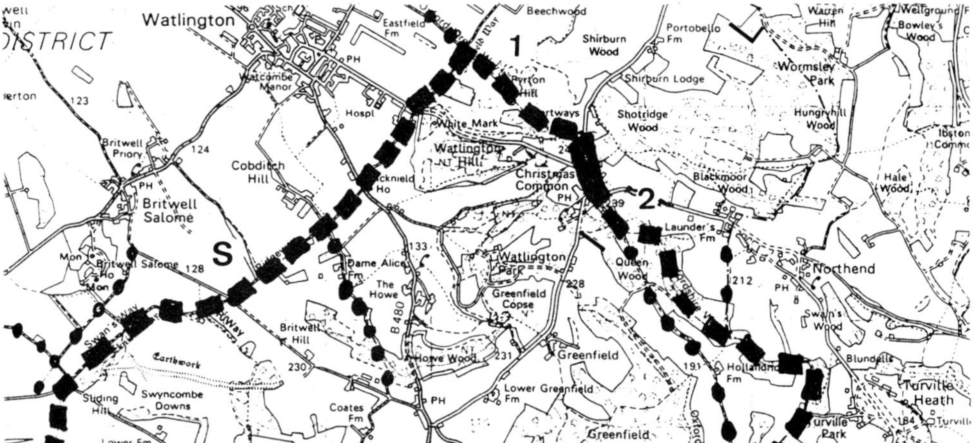

Route **15**:-CHRISTMAS COMMON & the CHILTERNS

CHRISTMAS COMMON & the CHILTERNS Route 15

17 miles, circular (clockwise)
Ordnance Survey maps:
Landranger 175;
Pathfinder "Chiltern Hills South".
Length:
17 miles (27 km) in total, of which
15 miles (23km) bridleway.
Several shorter alternatives.
Parking & starting point:

Road verge (GR.682922) 1 mile southeast of **Britwell Salome** (B4009 between Watlington & Benson) at the junction of the Ridgeway and the Britwell Salome to Britwell Hill road

Route description

Start. Follow the **Ridgeway** (a BOAT, here also "*Swan's Way*" and "*Icknield Way*") northeast for 2 miles. You cross over a farm road to **Dame Alice Fm**., over the busy B480 at **Icknield Ho**. (CARE) and then over a minor road (Watlington to Christmas Common).

1. Turn right along the bridleway signposted "Oxfordshire Way" (GR.703945). This leads southeast from Pyrton, past a sawmill and up a valley into the Chilterns (*splendid viewpoint at 242 m alt. over the Oxfordshire plain*). Turn right for 400 m along a minor road past a "T" road-junction to **Christmas Common.** Where the road forks *(50 m down the right fork is the "The Fox & Hounds"PH with a hitching rail Tel. 01234 567654*), bear left for 100 m to a bend in the road and enter Hollandridge Lane on your right (BOAT & bridleway).

2. After 400 m turn left, east, into a beechwood bridleway and then a winding valley-bottom track down to **Turville Park Fm**. The bridleway then leads through fields to a minor road (GR.736897) (1mile). Turn right, due south, for 300 m to the "T" road-junction at **Whitepond Farm.**

3. Turn left along the B480 (CARE), past **Stonor Park** *(deer park and Tudor mansion with its attached R.C. Chapel)* to a "T" road-junction at **Stonor** village. Turn right, due west, along a minor road rising up to **Maidensgrove** woods.

4. Turn left, before leaving the beechwoods, onto a steep bridleway which goes due south and leads to a cross-field bridleway into Lodge Farm (GR. 724884). Turn right from the farmyard, then immediately left into a BOAT track continuing due south through **Maidensgrove Scrubs**. At a viewpoint overlooking the BBONT **Nature Trail** take the right fork and go down the hillside into the valley (*containing* **Valley End Fm.** *& the remains of* **St. James' Church**). Turn right along the macadamed BOAT which winds north west to **Pages Fm. &** becomes a wooded track at the BBONT Warburg Reserve Centre. Continue along the valley bottom to a fork in open fields, where you go west into a lane which continues past **Westwood Manor Fm.** to a road fork at **Park Corner.**

5. Take the left fork at **Park Corner** and then turn right towards the B481 Nettlebed road (GR.694884). Cross (CARE), turn right along the road for 10 m, then turn left, immediately before a wooden barn, onto a green lane bridleway running west along the north edge of Hazel Wood. Continue west, dropping down into a wooded valley below the

HM. Young Offender Institution. After crossing a Ridgeway footpath, go down through Oakengrove Copse onto a track past a small farm and contour northwest through fields along **Harcourt Hill.**

6. When in line with **May's Farm** and a garage (away to your left & down on the A423) turn right due north along a field-edge bridleway. At a bridleway crossing, continue ahead on a hard track over **Ewelme Downs**.

7. Cross the tarmac road east of **Down Fm.** onto a field-edge bridleway going north to a minor road. Turn right again, northeast, and enter a green lane track ("Swan's Way / Icknield Way") along the edge of **Sliding Hill** beechwoods to return to the start.

Alternative routes/sections. **(A. B. C. D.)**

A.) Take the right fork at **Park Corner** (Point 5) and then turn second left to the B481 (GR. 692888). Cross (CARE) into a minor road opposite. After **Parkcorner Fm.** (Point 10) turn left, west, along a tree-lined bridleway approach to **Ewelme Park**. Continue ahead between the House and the Polo stables and ride down into open fields. At the bridleway crossing (Point 6), turn right along the hard track track over **Ewelme Downs** and past **Down Fm.** (Point 7, see para. 7 above).

B.) At the **Maidensgrove** bridleway crossing (Point 4), turn right onto a steep path which then contours round the beechwoods before going steeply down through Bury Wood. Cross over Stonor estate track onto a field edge bridleway and go due north up to **Pishill** *(O.E. 1195 "hill where the peas grow" with a rebuilt Norman Church).* Take the double-hedged bridleway on your left which curves up due west along a wood and leads into a track between farm buildings at **Russell's Water**. *(due south across the Common is "The Five Horseshoes" PH).* Continue west to the village duck pond, turn left south along the road for 100 m to the cottages at a triangular village green. Turn right at a former chapel into a lane which falls steeply into a wooded valley. At the track below, turn right to **Cookley Green** (1 km). Turn left under the trees on the village green lining the B481. Cross (CARE) into a minor road opposite (Point 9) going to Ewelme. After 1 mile, turn left to **Swyncombe House** *(with an 11.C Norman flint church).* Take the bridleway track into a wooded valley, first southwest then west. Contour along a field-edge bridleway to a spinney; then turn right on a tarmac road dropping to **Down Fm**. (Point 7, see para.7 above).

C.) From the Ridgeway (GR. 690928) near **Cobditch Hill** take a bridleway south past **Dame Alice Fm.** up into the woods. At a minor road, turn left for 400m. to the B481. Cross (CARE) and turn right using the road verge along the east side the B481 (CARE) for half a mile to **Cookley Green** (Point 9). N.B. THIS ROUTE **C.)** IS NOT RECOMMENDED IN THE OPPOSITE DIRECTION

D.) At **Christmas Common,** (Point 2) continue ahead along Hollandridge Lane (a BOAT) for 2 miles, passing **Hollandridge Fm**. Drop down to join the B480 then turn right and ride along the B480 (CARE) to **Pishill.** Turn first left to the church (Point 8). Take either the double-hedged bridleway up to your right to **Russells Water** or the field edge bridleway straight ahead going down and then up through Bury Wood to **Maidensgrove** (Point 4). [1]

BLEWBURY, COMPTON & EAST ILSLEY Route 16

One ride, 17 miles, circular (clockwise)
Four carriage drives, 6 to 10 miles.
Ordnance Survey maps:
Landranger 174,
Pathfinder 1155, 1171
Length (of ride):
17 miles (27 km) in total, of which
13 miles (21 km) bridleway, BOAT/RUPP.
Parking & starting points:-
(i) Blewbury Equestrian Centre, (please first tel. 01235 851016)
(ii) road verge, Churn Fm., Blewbury (GR.511833)
(iii) top of Kingstanding Hill Lane off A417, Moulsford (GR.573837)
(iv) Haydon La., a BOAT, nr. duckpond East Ilsley (GR.494810)
(v) road verge, Superity Fm., Compton (GR.515807)
(vi) "*Horse & Jockey*" PH. Downs Rd Clifton (large car park & restaurant, plse. tel. 01235 820811; cross A34 to village by A4185 flyover or by bridleway underpass).

Local interest.
*The downland on the county boundary has prehistoric roads, hillforts & fieldsystems, Roman burial grounds & temples, sections of Grim's Ditch, moated farms, racing stables and gallops - but virtually no gates. Like Lambourn to the west along the Ridgeway, it has a large network of public paths primarily used for riding and driving. In an area east of the A34 (of less than 20 sq. miles bounded by GR.490800, 570800, 490860 & 570860) the villages of **Blewbury, Aston Tyrold, Compton, E.Ilsley** and **Chilton** are linked by a dense off-road network of RUPPs or BOATS (32 miles), bridleways (11 m.) and footpaths (11 m.). Cleopatra-like, the alternative routes are of "infinite variety" and length.*

Route description (the ride)
1. From Blewbury Equestrian Centre turn right for 400 m along the B4016 (CARE). Turn left east along Winterbrook Fm. track into a field bridleway below **Blewburton Hill** *(Iron Age fort with remnants of a Lynchet field system)*. Turn left into a gravel track which winds past Granary Cottage (*on stone stilts*) and All Saints Church (*with its modest wooden steeple)* into Thorpe Lane, **Aston Upthorpe**. Turn right along Spring Lane for 400 m ("*The Chequers*" *PH. is up to your left in Fullers Road)* passing the United Reform Church (*founded in 1662, built in 1728*)
2. After a Queen Anne ho. & the Copse Stile Fm. barns, turn east into a short bridleway on your left leading to the adjoining village of **Aston Tirrold** *(together, they make only one pretty downland village with timbered & thatched houses and small churches*). The brookside gravel path ends as a residential driveway. Turn right along Baker St., Aston St. & Chalk Hill for 150 m to a tree-shaded green lane on your left which leads east to **Lollingdon Fm.**, (*an attractive moated house with redbrick buildings and, in spring, massed daffodils*). Follow the farm track as it turns south. At the **Cholsey** road, turn right for 800 m past **Westfield Stables** to the double "T" road-junction (Halfpenny La. & the A417 (GR. 573838).
3. Cross the A417 into **Kingstanding Hill** lane opposite (CARE, a crossing NOT recommended in the opposite direction). The wooded lane climbs up, west, to a car park on **Cholsey Downs** (124 m alt.). Continue southwest along **The Fair Mile**

(a wide, level, 1 mile 4 furlongs length of race track under the Stuarts).

4. At the bridleway junction turn left into the track up to **Lowbury Hill** (a *wooded site 186 m alt. with Roman tumulus* GR. 544826). After 200 m due south, take a right fork, again southwest, for 2 km. Cross the **Ridgeway** path at right angles (*alt.156 m, west of both Warren and Starveall Fms*) and continue downhill on "Berkshire Circular routes" to a wooded "Crows Foot" junction of five paths (GR. 534805).

5. Turn right, west, along a bridleway and then turn left under a disused railway bridge to Baxter's Healthcare, Wallingford Rd., **Compton**. Turn left at Roden Ho., then right at *"The Swan" PH.* and ride through the village. (**Superity Fm**. *is up "Churn Rd." the second road on the right).*

6. At the "T" road-junction (Hampstead Norreys to E.Ilsley) continue ahead for 100 m (CARE) to the bend (103 m alt). Turn left into "Cheseridge Rd" leading to "Warnham Lane". Ride past **Mayfield Fm**. up to Warnham's Cottages then turn right at the hilltop (160 m alt.) into a green lane going southwest. At the "T" path-junction in the valley, turn right, northwest, to cross "Dennisford Rd" track at right angles, on **Shrill Down.** Go down into **East Ilsley**, past the playground, school, church and duck pond to *"The Crown & Horns"* PH *(two stables & hitching rail shaded by twin chestnut trees; Tel.01635 281205/545*).

7. Take the road towards the A34 but turn off right after 100 m at Ashdown Cottage into a lane and a fieldedge bridleway rising up to the Ridgeway on **Several Down**. Cross the gallops dogleggedly, right then left, going northeast across **Compton Downs** down to a bridge over the **dismtd rly** (GR.510832) on **Blewbury Down.**

8. Use the "Boham's Rd" track for 500 m due north, turning right along the entrance to **Churn Fm.** Turn left onto the bridleway going northeast below the *tumulus* at **Churn Knob** to the A417 at **Blewbury**.

9. Cross the A417 (CARE) into "Westbrook St." opposite. Go round the western and northern edges of the village (a stream appears on your left) to the B4016 at Winterbrook Fm. Go left along the road (CARE) to return to the Start.

25 A Party outside an Inn, 1699

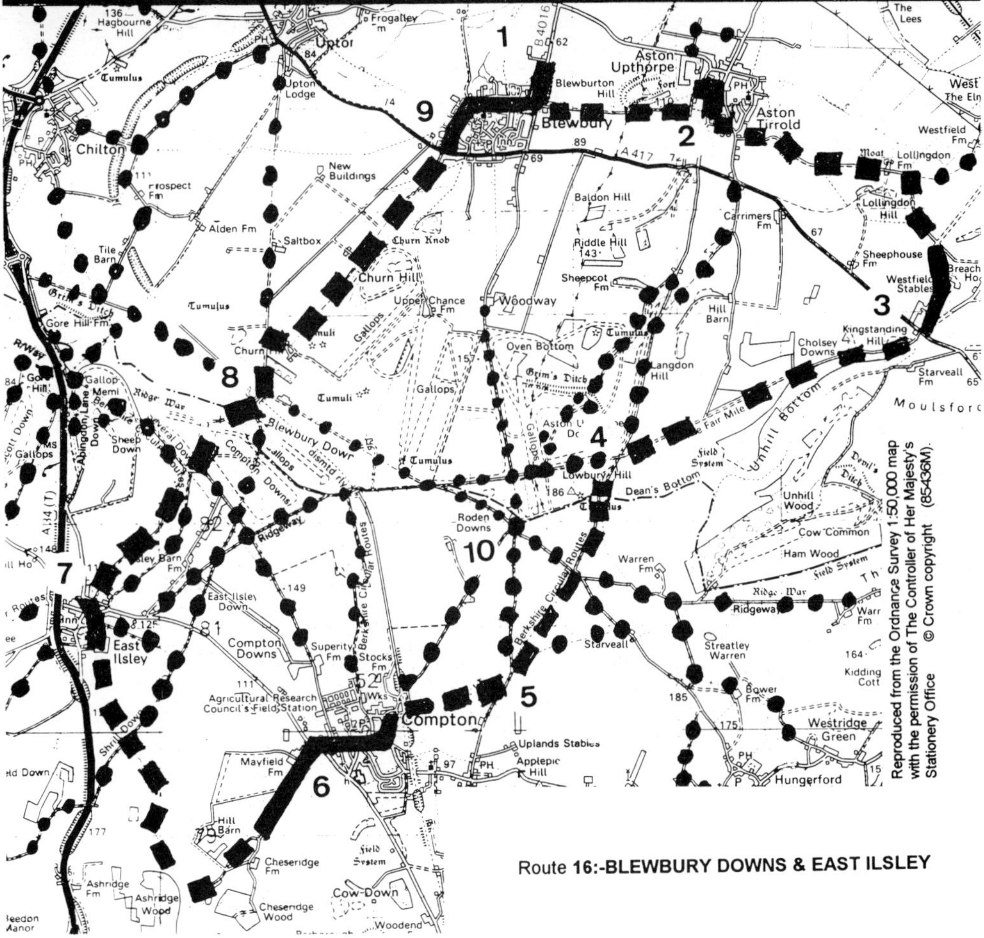

Route **16:-BLEWBURY DOWNS & EAST ILSLEY**

Four routes for carriage drivers.

(Note: *Some sections are concrete or gravel roads, others are rutted farm tracks more suited to cross-country carriages. They are therefore shorter than the ride*).

A1.) From Blewbury Equestrian Centre, turn left for 500 m then right along "Hagbourne Rd" to **Aston Upthorpe.** Turn right to wind past racing stables and All Saints Church in Thorpe Lane, then right again into Spring Lane (Point 2) and pass the United Reform Church going due south to the A417. Cross (CARE) into the track opposite. After 1 km at Chalk Hill Bottom barn, fork left due south and climb up to the **Fair Mile** track (Point 4). Turn right, west, below **Lowbury Hill**, crossing gallops & the Woodway/Roden Downs track (right angles). Join the **Ridgeway** briefly but fork right northwest on level ground to **Churn Fm**. (Point 8). Take "Boham's Rd" northeast to **Blewbury**. Turn right (CARE) on the A417 for 150m., turn left into Westbrook St. round the village to the B4016 and the Start. (10 miles, 16 km)

A2.) After **Lowbury Hill** and crossing the gallops, turn right due north along the Woodway/Roden Downs track, past **Woodway** stables then down a steep road to **Blewbury**. At the Elf Garage, cross the A417 (CARE) into B4016 opposite back to the Start (7.5 miles, 12 km).

B.) From **Churn Fm**. (Point 8), go due north, past **Saltbox**, to join the **Alden Fm**. track and go down to the A417 at **Upton**. Turn left for 50 m (CARE) to enter the "Lynch Way", a RUPP "Carttrack" by the "*George & Dragon*" PH. At a "T" path-junction before **Prospect Fm**. turn right, west, to Dene Hollow & Lime Trees Road, **Chilton**. Turn left by the church, bearing right at Place Fm. Go south to a road (*and to the "Rose & Crown" PH*) leading into a track, parallel to the A34, which rises then drops down to join a gravelled track below **Gore Hill Fm**. Turn left, southeast, on a green lane track heading south east for the bridge over the **dsmtld rly** by **Churn Fm**. (6.5 miles, 10 km).

C.) From **Superity Fm**., go northwest along the concrete track to the right-angle crossing where the Ridgeway joins. Continue ahead, gradually climbing up to **Several Downs** (171 m alt.) and then the tunnel under the A34 on **Gore Hill** (see also map for Route 17). Cross the West Ilsley road car park (1 km.) on **Bury Down** and turn off the Ridgeway at **East Hendred Down** (2 km). The track drops down due northeast, past Ridgeway Fm paddocks, **Rutherford Lab.** and **Upper Fm**. to the "*Horse & Jockey*" PH. Downs Rd, **Chilton**. At the garden centre, turn right (CARE) along the A4185 for 300 m over the A34 and right again to the "*Rose & Crown*" PH, the road and then the track heading southeast to **Churn Fm** (Point 8). Turn right before the rly bridge and then fork left up the track rising across **Compton Downs** & gallops to the Ridgeway. Turn left, southeast back to the Start (10 miles, 16 km).[1]

CHILTON, WEST ILSLEY & W. LOCKINGE Route 17

19 miles, circular (clockwise)
Ordnance Survey maps:
Landranger 174
Pathfinder 1115
Length:
19 miles (30 km) in total, of which
16 miles (25 km) bridleway.
Many alternatives.

Parking & starting points:
(i) Road verge, near *"Horse & Jockey"* PH (tel. 01235 820811) adjacent to the Garden Centre; Downs Road, **Chilton,** turning south onto the A4185 from the A417 (GR. 486/860):-
(ii) Ridgeway Farm Livery, Chilton (plse. tel. Sarah Saunders 01235 821137), past the *"Horse & Jockey"PH.* taking a BOAT southwest past **Harwell Labs. &** **Upper Fm**. (GR. 468854)

Route description

Start. Where the road turns right going up between paddocks to Ridgeway Farm (or continues ahead as a rising grassy track), turn left onto a grass bridleway going due south, then southeast across **Chilton Downs** to twin roundabouts over the A34. Cross (CARE) towards Blewbury Downs, but turn south taking the bridleway road beside the A34 leading to **Gore Hill Fm.** Continue on a bridleway climbing steeply up to the Ridgeway. Turn right, go west under the A34 (tunnel).

1. At the first bridleway on your left, go due south alongside racing gallops, then fork right at a copse. Drop steeply down a gravel track to **West Ilsley.** Turn right, west, for 300 m along the road past the village shop & *"Harrow Inn" PH.(Tel.0165 281260).*

2. Turn right into a bridleway, at first a farmtrack and then a grassy path, which goes northwest steeply up on perfect turf alongside **Sheep Down** racing gallops. Rejoin the Ridgeway at **East Hendred Down** *(the junction of several paths with panoramic views at 187 m alt.).*

3. Turn left and follow the Ridgeway west for 1 km to the woodland on the horizon. Take the rights of way track by *a* small car park and a large Information board which is just east of Fore Down woods (*which hide* **Scutchamer Knob** *alias Cuckhamsley Hill, a Saxon burial ground, Cwichelmeshlaew, c.636*).

4. Turn left off the Ridgeway onto a grass track due south besides gallops for 1/2 mile, then bear right south west between a fence and a hedge to a minor road (Farnborough to W. Isley). Turn right along the road for 300 m down to **Lands End** (GR. 447833).

5. Where a bridleway crosses the road, turn right then left onto the lower of two tracks behind the house. The track, in a gently rising valley, invites a sustained canter up to **Wether Down** back to the Ridgeway.

6. Turn left along the Ridgeway and where the widening track curves south west to **Wantage Monument** (*a prominant Victorian memorial*), bear right under trees and continue west down below **Grim's Ditch** (*the Devil's Ditch in Saxon*). At the Gallops, turn right along the west edge, going due north, then northeast onto the track (two cattle-grids) which passes **Arn Hill** (a *Saxon burial mound 129 m above sea level*) into **West Lockinge**.

7. At the minor road, turn right to **East Lockinge.** *(You now enter a sheltered valley with elegant houses, gardens, racing stables and parkland).* Bear left at the monument, go down past the church and trout steam (on your left) then bear right passing in turn **Betterton Ho.**, a "T" road-junction and then **Betterton Farm.**

8. After the "S" road bend at **West Ginge**, but before the racing stables at **East Ginge**, enter the bridleway on your right. A green lane between hedges leads steeply up to the open downs. At the Ridgeway, turn left to **Scutchamer Knob** (Point 4) and **East Hendred Down** (Point 3). Turn left off the Ridgeway by the track leading down northeast and return to **Chilton** (Ridgeway Farm Livery is up on your left).

Alternative routes.

A.) At **East Lockinge** (Point 7), turn left, north into a road rising to **Ardington** and then turn right at a sharp bend onto a BOAT going due east (often a muddy track) for 4 km to **Aldfield Common &** the perimeter fence of **Harwell.** Turn right and follow this fence round to Ridgeway Farm and back to Chilton.

B.) At **East Lockinge** (Point 7) continue 400 m further on the road to **Ginge** and take a fieldedge bridleway on the left going north rising steeply up over the hill (two hunting gates) and then dropping down to the same BOAT crossing at right-angles (GR. 436875) by **Roundabout Hill**. *(The bridleway continues north past* ***Sheephouse Fm.*** *into Ardington. Turn left by Ardington Ho. to "The Boar's Head"PH. tel. 01235 833254).*

C.) From the Lockinge to Ginge road, take the hard, all-weather farm track past **Betterton Fm.** which climbs, east of **Droveway Hill**, back up to the Ridgeway.

To shorten or to lengthen the routes in this area,, a veritable Pandora's Box of connected rights of way can be further opened by using the BHS "*Ridgeway Downs on Horseback*" (especially trails No. 2, 7, 14 & 15).[1]

GREAT FOLKS IN THE PARK.

A FARMER'S FAMILY ON HORSEBACK.

Route 17:-CHILTON, WEST ILSLEY & WEST LOCKINGE

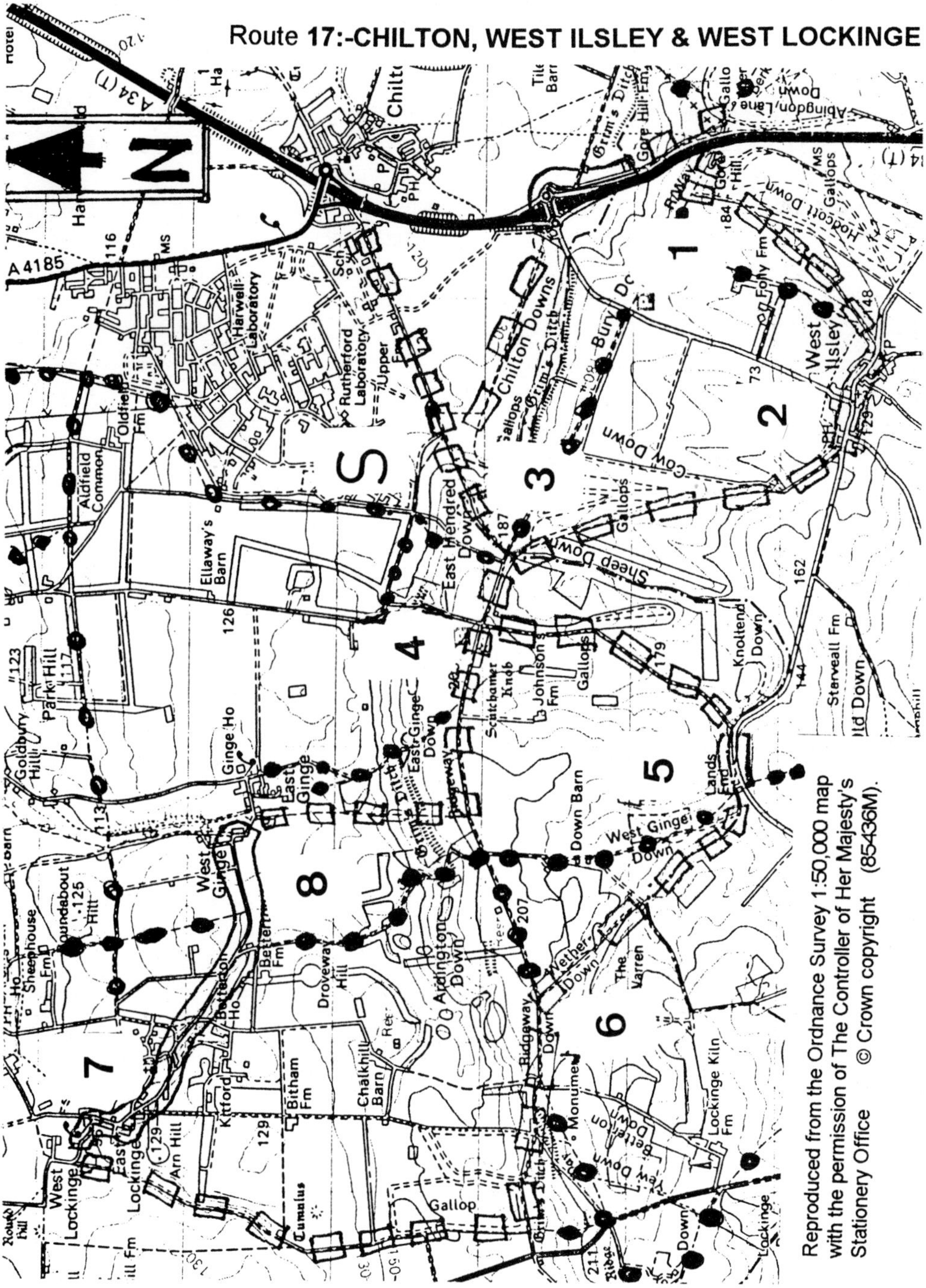

Reproduced from the Ordnance Survey 1:50,000 map with the permission of The Controller of Her Majesty's Stationery Office © Crown copyright (85436M).

The WHITE HORSE, WAYLANDS SMITHY & "TUNS"
Route 18

15 miles, circular (clockwise)
Ordnance Survey maps:
Landranger 174,
Pathfinder 1154
Length:
15 miles (24 km) in total, of which
10 miles (16 km) bridleway.
Shorter and longer alternatives.

Parking & starting point:
Start and Park:. "*The White Horse*" PH car park; **Woolstone**, (GR.293878) (please tel. 01367 820726). From Watchfield four miles south of Faringdon on the A420, take the B4508 for 1 km; then the road to Uffington & Woolstone.

Interest

The 374 ft long **Uffington** *White Horse and Hill Fort, near the highest, most northerly, section of the Ridgeway, demonstrate the prestige and power of our Iron Age pre-historic ancestors who used this east/west chalk ridge as an all-weather trading route above the wooded Thames valley marshes. Eight sheltered Oxfordshire villages lie within a mile of each other and of the Ridgeway whereas Berkshire to the south has only Lambourn 5 miles away. Sixteen place-names on or near this ride have as suffix either "ton/tone" from the Old English "tûn" for "farm", "settlement" etc. or "bury" for a "fort". The Doomsday Book lists Ashbury as "Eissieberie".*

Route description

Start. Ride south up the road to the B4507 "T" road-junction. Cross into the lane opposite and turn left immediately into a field bridleway (*a permissive path dedicated by the National Trust NT)* which climbs steeply beside the narrow road up to the landscaped car park on **Woolstone Hill.** Turn south after the second gate and traverse left across the open hill to cross a metalled NT road where a bridleway rises steeply up to the left shoulder of **Uffington Hill** fort. *(The Horse itself is not visible from this 261 m viewpoint; but in the foreground is the mound where St.George slew the Dragon and in the distance are the Cotswold and Chiltern Hills*).

1. Turn south through a bridleway gate onto the **Ridgeway** BOAT (GR.303863) and turn right, south west for 7 km along the undulating Ridgeway. Cross over the **Woolstone** and the **Knighton** tracks, to see **Waylands Smithy** in a clump of beech trees 100 m to your right *(A hitching rail here would allow a visit by Shank's Pony to the Saxon farrier and a well-restored 180 ft. Long Barrow*).

2. Cross first the **Odstone** track and then the B4000 metalled road (Ashbury to Lambourn).

3. At the **Idstone** track crossing, *(201 m alt.),* with barns beside the Ridgeway, a water trough on the right is very welcome on a hot day *(*GR.264835). Continue to another metalled road crossing (Bishopstone to Russley Downs) at **Ridgeway Fm.** and climb again up past **Charlbury Hill** (*another hill fort 253 m alt.*) towards **Fox Hill** *(surmounted by a prominant radio mast on your left. Some 400 m straight on & lower down is "The Shepherd's Rest" PH strategically placed at the cross roads of pre-historic Ridgeway and Roman Ermine Street.).* Turn right off the Ridgeway opposite a corrugated iron

Route **18:-The WHITE HORSE, WAYLAND's SMITHY and the "TUNS"**

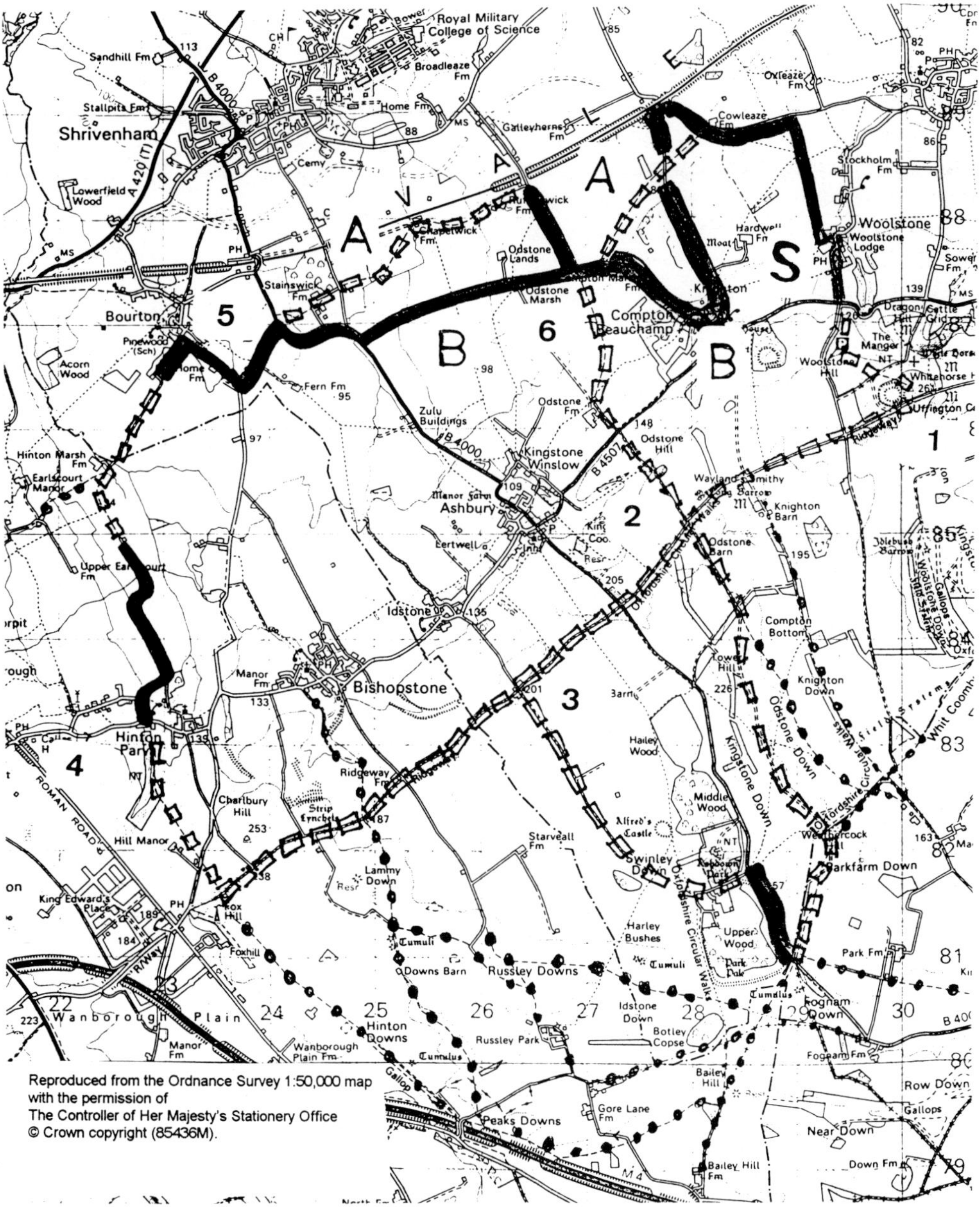

Reproduced from the Ordnance Survey 1:50,000 map with the permission of The Controller of Her Majesty's Stationery Office barn down into a field bridleway going northwest.. Cross a minor road and go between **Hill Manor** racing stables on your left and their gallops on your right. Go north steeply down beside a deep valley (*National Trust*) into a car park behind the old chapel at **Hinton Parva**.

4. Take the road immediately opposite for 200 m to "City Corner" & continue on a metalled lane which curves right to a "T" road-junction. Turn left and continue zigzagging north onto a grassed bridleway track to **Hinton Marsh Fm.** Traverse two small paddocks and a stream gateway south of the farmhouse onto a farm road going northeast to **Bourton.** At **Pinewood School**, turn right along the Bishopstone Road, past St. James' Church and **Home Fm**. then turn first left to the B4000.

5. Choose either 5(A) or 5(B), according to recent weather.

5(A) If dry, cross the B4000 (CARE) to a bridleway 20 m left, which goes northeast through seven low-lying fields of **Stainswick, Chapelwick and Ruffinswick Fms** *(the Saxon word "wick" denotes an agricultural, cottage industry or monastic settlement*). At the minor road, turn right south east for 1 km to a "T" road-junction.

5(B) If wet, turn right along the B4000 for 700 m (CARE); and then turn second left into a BOAT going due east to the above "T" road-junction. Go east on the road for 200 m towards **Compton Marsh Fm**. (GR.274875).

6. Choose either 6(A) or 6(B), according to recent weather.

6(A) If dry; before **Compton Marsh Fm.**, take a field bridleway on your left going northeast. Cross a minor road to a cross-field bridleway leading to **Cowleaze Fm**.

6(B) If wet; continue past **Compton Marsh Fm**. on a long detour southeast via **Compton Beauchamp** *(a fine 16 C to 18C moated manor house*) and **Knighton**. Then go north west to "T" road junction at the railway and turn right past **Cowleaze Fm** for 700 m. east. At a "T" road junction, turn right again due south for 1km. along the road (good verge) back to **Woolstone**.

Alternatives.

Of the numerous bridleways/BOATS south of the Ridgeway, the following figure-of-eight route is interesting (12 miles).

At the **Idstone** barn and water trough junction (Point 3) (GR.264835), turn left down a track southeast to **Ashdown House** (*a 17 C NT. house "consecrated" to Elizabeth, beautiful daughter of James I, later the "Winter Queen" of Bohemia, widowed in 1632 and consoled for 30 years by Lord Craven, wealthy supporter of her husband King Frederick V, of her brother Charles I and of her nephew Charles II, for whom he financed the Coldstream Guards*). Turn right along the B4000 for 1 km and then turn left onto a 5 km bridleway, which goes north to **Weathercock Hill** (on the Berkshire boundary) and then forks left, northwest and north, up **Odstone Down.** Cross the Ridgeway (Point 2) and go down to the B4507. Enter the **Odstone Farm** road opposite, (*marked "D'Arcy Dalton Way" to commemorate a University don and long serving President of the Oxford & District Footpath, Bridleways & Commons Society).* Turn right by the white farm cottages into a field bridleway going first northeast then north across three fields to the "T" road-junction by **Compton Marsh Fm**. (Point 6). Follow para.6 above back to the start.[1]

MASTER AND GROOM.

STOKE ROW & the MAHARAJAH Route 19

14 miles, circular (clockwise)

Ordnance Survey maps:
Landranger 175
Pathfinder 1156

Length :
14 miles (23 km) in total, of which
11 miles (17 km) bridleway.
Several alternatives.

Parking & starting point:
(i) On village green (or ask permission at the *"Cherry Tree"* PH) **Stoke Row**, near Checkendon, off the A4074, 5 miles SE Wallingford (GR.683839).
(ii) in a shaded side road, near **Newnham Fm** (GR.618885) **Mongewell Park**, 500 m SW of the Crowmarsh Gifford roundabout (A423 & A4074) (Point 8) or in a redundant section of the A4074. Then join this route near **Woodhouse Fm**. (Point 5)

Of Interest

A *brick & pottery industry started at* **Stoke Row** *in the 1600s and clay pits are visible opposite the village hall (alt. 204 m). After a drought, a 365 ft deep, twin-bucketed, well, housed in a handsome cupola, with a warden's cottage and cherry orchard, was donated in 1864 by the Maharajah of Benares, where Mr. A. Edward Reade was then Lieut.-Governor, North-West Provinces. The latter had previously donated a well to improve an Indian village water supply, together with a house and a mango orchard for its maintenance. His epitaph is "Be not weary of welldoing". His brother Charles, also born at Ipsden House which he called 'the coldest house in Europe', is remembered by the humanitarian concern in his novels & plays about conditions in mental asylums, prisons and "coffin ships").*

Route description

Start from the village green at **Stoke Row.** Turn north along a local road to the corner of **Bush Wood** (*"The Crooked Billet" PH is just to your left*). Turn right onto a bridleway going through beech woods southeast on high ground. Drop down to a minor road (from Stoke Row to **Witheridge Hill**) and cross onto the bridleway opposite which climbs up into **Bear Wood**. At a gap in the forestry fence, turn right and go south to join a forest track. After another bridleway joins from the left, turn right just before the *"Grouse & Claret"* PH on the west side of **Kingwood Common**.

1. Cross the minor road into the bridleway lane opposite, going southwest through woods. Cross over the lamp-lit, local road (which is the entrance to the former **Borocourt Hospital** on your right), onto a field bridleway. Cross a minor road into the mixed stand of beech and rhododendrons opposite and immediately bear right inside the wood, heading southwest. At the next minor road, cross into a woodland bridleway track going along the southern edge of **Nippers Grove.** Cross another minor road into a field bridleway opposite.

2. Before the A4074, at a cottage and a "bodger's" barn (*where a craftsman makes traditional besoms and hurdles*), turn right due north along a wooded track to **Hook End**. Turn left on the road for 1 km.

3. Take the right road fork at **Lower Fm** *(where a bridleway on the right returns through woods to Stoke Row past the Forestry Commission site in Ipsden Wood).* Turn left at the entrance to **Corker's Fm.** along a bridleway track going northwest

through woods and then through fields to the Checkenden to Woodcote road. Turn left along this road for 100 m (CARE) and turn off right into a macadamed road at the western edge of **Checkenden Court**. Continue west, past **Hammond's Fm**. entrance, on a forest track which drops down through beech woods and then along a green road into the valley (*Note the terrassed strip lynchets on the hillside opposite*). Turn left along the road, pass **Ousely Barn** and fork right going due north. Pass the entrance to **Braziers Park.**

4. At the next cross-roads, turn left due west to a "T" road-junction by Ipsden Farm, with its 18 C. Great Barn (*the longest in the county & built for barley harvests*) and just opposite, its brick and tile grain store on raised stone supports. Turn left for 400 m. Enter right the green lane bridleway running due north for 2 km (*this is the prehistoric "Icknield Way"*). Cross a minor road (Ipsden to North Stoke) and go northeastwards on a field bridleway below **Cobler's Hill** to a road fork by **Wicks'Hill** and **Drunkard's Bottom.**

5. Choose 5(A) or 5(B).

5(A) Take the righthand fork north up the hill and turn right, east, into the lane to **Woodhouse Fm.** Follow a track bridleway by **Wicks Wood**, keeping the fence to your left up a winding grass track to **Bachelor's Hill** and through **Mongewell Woods** onto open land (alt. 200 m). Cross the Nuffield road into the lane opposite and keep straight on into a drive signposted **Whitcalls Fm**. Continue past a modern, 20 C country house on high ground to your right, down to Oakingham Bottom and a narrow valley in **Bush Woods**. Where a bridleway crosses the lane, turn right to climb steeply up the beechwoods and exit at a road bend (to the right is *"The Crooked Billet"* PH). Turn left to return to the village green.

5(B) Turn sharp right, southeast, along the road for 1 km, towards **Ipsden** (*"Yppesdene" 1086 DB, OE. meaning "valley near the upland"*). After **Poors Fm**, at the "T" junction, take the left turn to **Hailey.** Pass the "*King William*" PH. (*proudly offering NO food but an interesting collection of rural hand tools*) on a lane which becomes a woodland track climbing east up to **Bixmoor Wood**. Continue on the winding track past **Homer Fm** and cross the Nuffield road (CARE) into the lane opposite which becomes a green lane and drops down after 1 mile to **Stoke Row Fm**. A macadamed road leads to the cherry orchard and the Maharajah's Well in **Stoke Row**. Turn left along the road to return to the village green.

Extra routes

The "Judges Ride" (16 miles), published by the O.C.C. as a free leaflet, goes from **Stoke Row**, via **Ipsden Heath, Well Place Zoo, Warren Hill,** to Point 5, Point 4, across the A4074 to Point 6, across the B4009 to Point 7 and **North Stoke,** thence to **Mongewell Park** (Point 8) and returns back across the A4074 via 5(A) to Stoke Row.[1]

Route **19:-STOKE ROW & the MAHARAJAH's Ride**

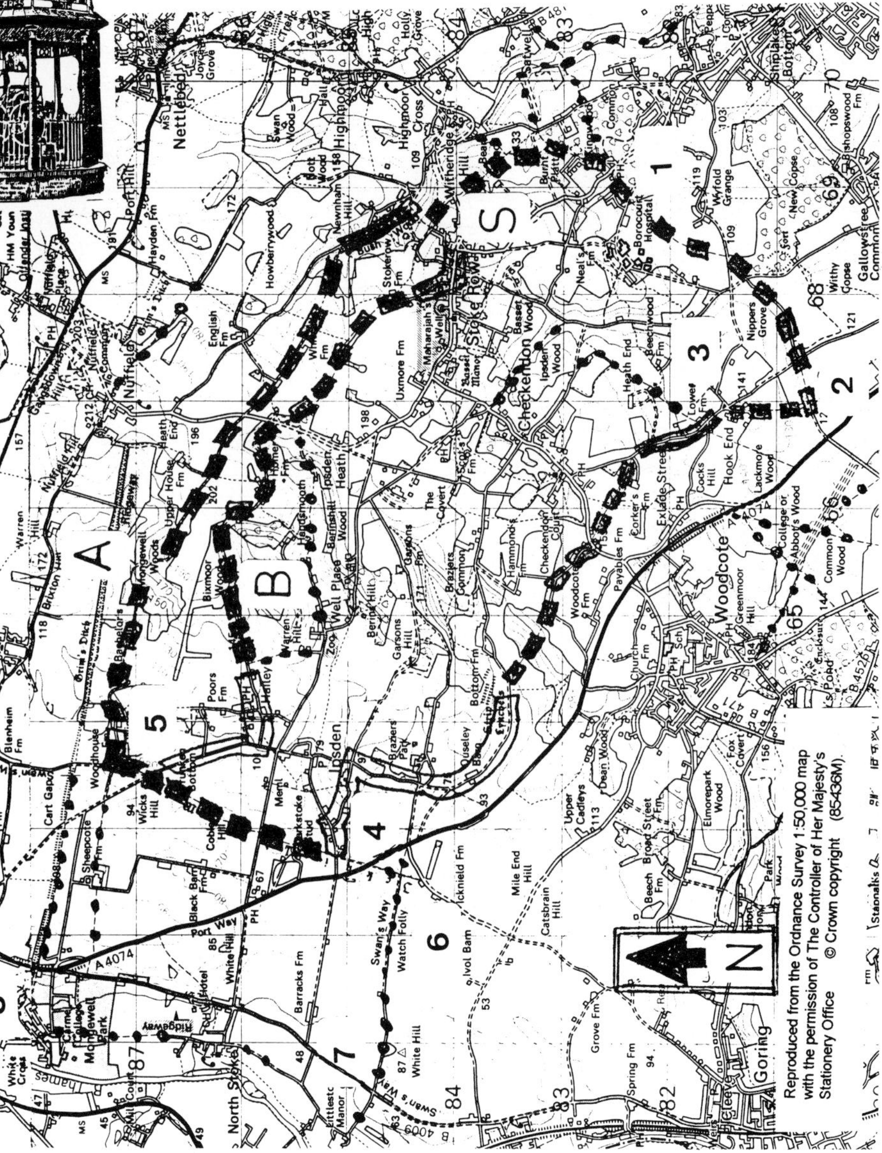

WARBOROUGH, WATLINGTON & EWELME

Route 20

18 miles, circular (anti-clockwise)
Ordnance Survey maps:
Landranger 164, 165,
Pathfinder 1137
Length: "The Great Circle" Route
18 miles (28 km) in total, of which
13 miles (20 km) bridleway.

Parking & starting point:

(i) Lower Berrick Farm, (Sue Clayton, tel. 01865 891073) (GR.619949) **Berrick Salome** 2 miles north of **Benson** on B4009
(ii) On the village green (GR.599937) at **Warborough** on the A329.

Route description

Start. Go north from **Berrick Salome** *(a manorial affix from the 13 C de Suleham family of Sulham Berkshire, DB Soleham "homestead by a gully")* for 250 m to **Berrick Prior**. Opposite "*The Chequers Inn*" PH (parking, Ian Wadham, plse. tel. 01865 891279) take the bridleway left, on a gravelled lane past houses, to a gate into open fields. Bear left, southwest, across the first field to a high, narrow metal gate; turn right then left along the edge of the second field following a ditch, southwest. Cross over two wooden bridges by a plantation onto an avenue of poplars & a green lane bridleway leading to **Warborough**, *(O.E.* meaning *"Watch Hill"*).

1. Turn left at the splendid village green & sports field, (*records from 1860 link the cricket club with the "Cricketers", "Nags Head", "Six Bells", "Kingfisher" or the "Shillingford Bridge" PHs with the motto:-*

"Win or lose, we enjoy our booze").

Go past the allotments, and turn left into a lane which goes east across open fields with two concrete bridges to a "T" road-junction.. Take the road opposite for 300 m to **Roke**. Turn right at the *"Home, Sweet Home"* PH for 500 m to the B4009. Cross (CARE) and enter the green lane bridleway in a spinney going due south for 300 m.

2. Turn left for 600 m along the road by Benson Airfield to **Ewelme** *(meaning "River source". You can just see remnants of watercressbeds from a once extensive rural industry).* Turn left over the river then right by "*The Shepherd's Hut*" PH, along the village street, past the village duckpond to the 15 C church. *(East Anglian in architecture, with a magnificent font canopy and an elaborate tomb to Alice Chaucer, grand-daughter of Geoffrey and wife of John de la Pole, Earl of Suffolk. Jerome K. Jerome is buried in the graveyard. Dame Alice lived at Ewelme and donated the adjoining quadrangled almshouses for 13 men who fought at Agincourt in 1415 and below them a school, the oldest in the State system).*

3. Opposite the school, turn right and ride up the road to **Rabbit's Hill**. At the top right-hand bend, take the bridleway on the left which traverses the gravel quarry between fences to a minor road (where a second bridleway joins from the right). Cross the minor road into a green lane bridleway opposite going southeast. Where the lane ("*Swans Way*") bends right to **Potters Fm**, turn left into a spinney. At a bridleway junction, take the right hand fork continuing southeast as a hedge-row bridleway to open fields. At a bridleway cross-roads, turn left, due north below **Ewelme Downs** on a hard track which crosses a metalled road, east of **Down Fm.** and continues as a field-edge bridleway for

Route 20:-WARBOROUGH, WATLINGTON & EWELME

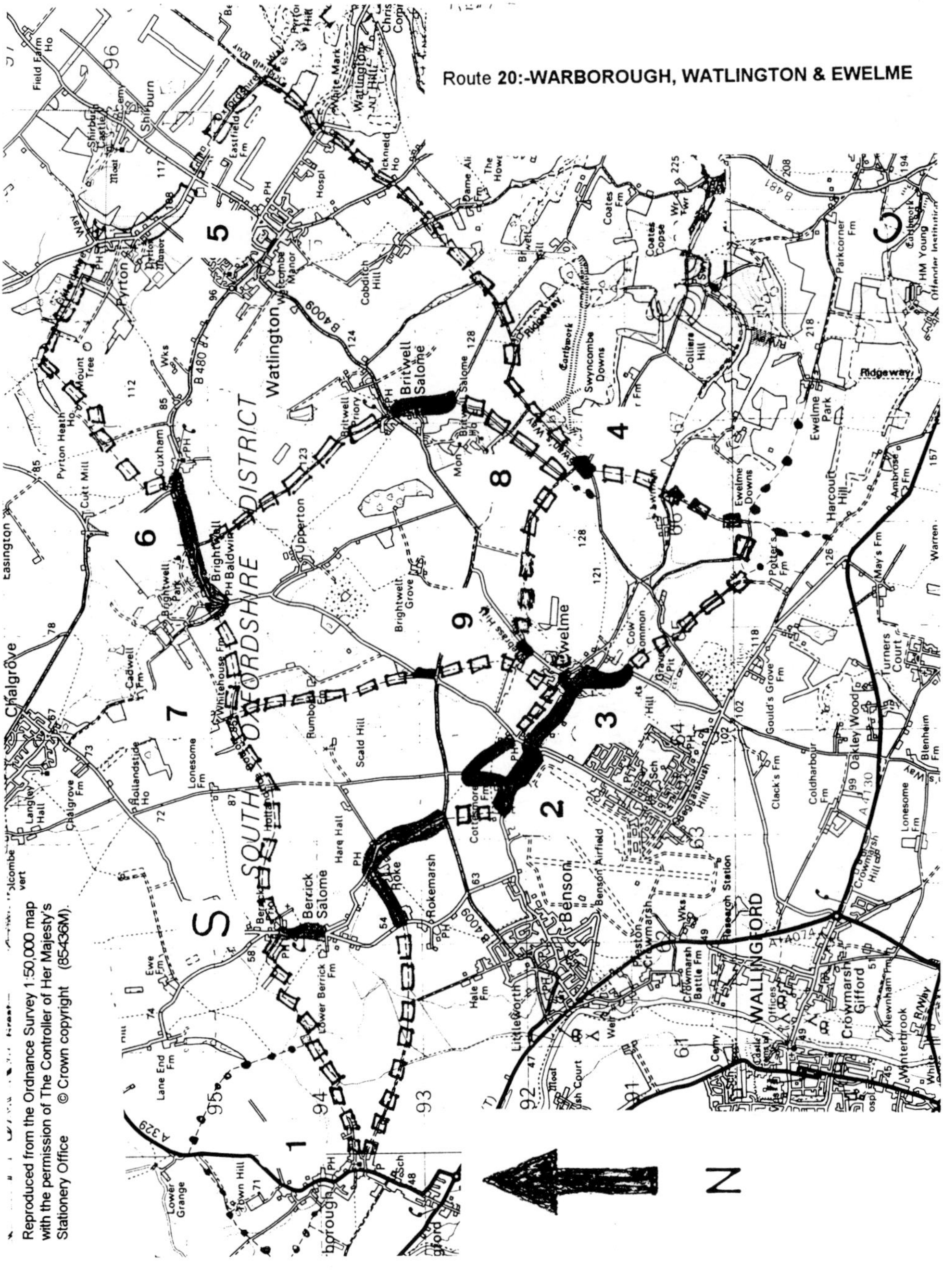

two fields to a metalled road which is followed for 50 m to the southwest corner of **Swyncombe Downs** beechwoods.

4. Where the road swings right (and rises up to the 11 C. Church at Swyncombe House & Cookley Green), take the green lane *BOAT* track ahead which continues northeast for 5 km. (*This is simultaneously the "Icknield Way", the "Ridgeway" and "Swans Way"*). You cross over two minor roads (Britwell Salome to Cookley Green and Cobditch Hill to **Dame Alice Fm.**). The third road at **Icknield Ho.** is the busy B480 (Watlington to Nettlebed). Cross (CARE). Some 700 m further on, where the "Oxfordshire Way" track crosses (coming down Christmas Common on the right), turn left northwest along a lane.

5. At the B4009, cross (CARE) into the minor road opposite leading past the manor into **Pyrton** village (*The name is O.E. for "pear orchard*"). Bear right to the "*The Plough*" PH and turn left almost immediately afterwards into a farm track bridleway which goes northwest along a wood and turns sharply southwest to **Pyrton Heath Ho**. The bridleway goes along the outside border of the garden, between the tennis court and the hedge and then turns sharp left onto a concrete drive with telegraph poles. At a bend in the drive, continue straight ahead southwest across one field bridleway to a hedge where the track goes left, south, to a willow-lined stream at **Cuxham** ("*The Half Moon*" PH tel. 01491 614110 is to your left). Turn right along the B480 for 50 m and turn off left into the **Brightwell Baldwin** road.

6. Pass a vineyard and "*The Lord Nelson Inn*" (car park, tel. 01491 612497) on your left and **Brightwell Park** and the church on your right. Turn right into a lane north for 100 m, then turn left into a bridleway lane which goes due west.

7. Where this fieldedge bridleway becomes a green lane (and is joined near **Whitehouse Fm.** by a twin-hedged bridleway coming north from Ewelme), continue due west along **"Hollandtide Bottom**". The lane crosses only one minor road before **Berrick Prior** (2 miles). Turn left, south, by road to the Start.

<u>Alternative routes</u> use parts of the above "Great Circle" route:-

a) Ride No.1 in the O.C.C *Recreational Routes* series (total length 13 miles, of which 9 miles bridleways) goes clockwise from Ewelme to Point 8, then to Britwell Salome, crosses the B4009 (CARE two traffic mirrors are placed at a blind bend) to Point 6, east to Pyrton, then Point 5, & southeast to Point 4 back to Ewelme.

b) A southwards link (4 km) between Point 6 and Point 8 provides a safer crossing of the B4009 at Britwell Salome. From the corner of Brightwell Baldwin Park, take "Turners Green Lane" south to the B4009 and a waiting area on the convex side of the bend at **Britwell Salome**. Cross (PATIENCE & CARE) into the road opposite by the "*Red Lion*" PH. Follow the road out of the village (verge) to a hard gravelled track going south west below the **Ho** and **Mon.** to Swincombe beechwoods.

c) A link (2 km) between Points 8 and 9. Turn right uphill along the gravelled pigfarm track to a fieldedge BOAT going west. At **Firebrass Hill**, turn left down the road for 30 m into a path through the spinney on your right for 200 m to a bridleway crossing (Point 9).

d) A link (3 km) between Points 9 and 7. At the two **Ewelme** woods (GR.646921), turn right on a field bridleway which bends left on rising ground due north to the B4009. Cross (CARE) into the minor road opposite signposted to Brightwell Baldwin.

After 100 m, go left at a spinney into a green lane bridleway past **Rumbold's Fm.** to join "**Hollandtide Bottom**" (Point 7).

e) To avoid aircraft on **Benson Airfield**, after 200 m on the Benson to Ewelme road turn left into **Cottesmore** Lane (Point 2), then turn right, southeast, on a minor road to a "T" road-junction just above ***"The Shepherd's Hut"*** PH. Cross (CARE) into a field-edge bridleway. At the houses and converted barns, turn first left, northeast, to a field bridleway going between paddocks to Firebrass Hill woods (Point 9).

f) At the **Ewelme** duck pond, turn left up Cat Lane. Before a sharp and steep bend in the road, turn left into Chaucer's Close, again left before the houses and right by converted barns to the woods (Point 9).[1]

Robin's ride to roman Dorchester — Ride 21

12 miles, linear
Ordnance Survey maps:
Landranger 151, Pathfinder 1161
Length (out & return):
24 miles (38 km) in total, of which
18 miles (29 km) bridleway.
Two shorter alternatives.
Parking & starting points:
a) Shotover Country Park (GR.570060), approach from Wheatley or Headington;
b) The Green (GR.565990), Marsh Baldon. by "*Seven Stars* " PH (tel. 01865 343255), 1 km east of A423 at Nuneham Courtney;
c) "No Exit" road at crossroads (GR.576948) by Bishop's Court Dorchester
Of interest
The route was the first stage of the 1995 1500 km ride by Robin Cleminson from Oxford through France to Barcelona to raise £30,000 for charity (including CLIC - "Cancer and Leukaemia in Childhood"). Robin left Shotover House, Wheatley with full camping gear and his Arab mare "Nellie", who later proved to be in foal.
The route can be started from either end, or from Marsh Baldon, as here described, dividing the route approximately into half.

> *March Baldon, Toot Baldon,*
> *Baldon in between,*
> *Big Baldon, Little Baldon,*
> *Baldon on the Green."*

Route description

1. Northwards from **Marsh Baldon** (*a Saxon village where St Peter's Church was built by the monks from Dorchester Abbey and has 14 C glass in the east window, an unusual, octagonal tower and a Jacobean pulpit with sounding board*). Follow the Romans up **Pebble Hill** at the northeast corner of the 24 acre, gated village green. The road leads into a bridlepath which passes **Baldon Row** and gives onto a minor road. Continue north for 250 m.

2. Take the bridleway track on the left, by New Farm, where the road bends right to **Toot Baldon** (*: "Toot" means "lookout"; here from 98 m altitude*). Enter the field gate and follow the right hand field-edge path down two fields to the east corner of Sandford Brake wood **(El. sub Stn)**. Continue north along a spinney and then on a surfaced road to the end of the wood.

3. Turn right, due east, across two fields. At the Watlington Road (B480), turn right for 50 m (verge) and cross (CARE) into the bridleway opposite, Kiln Lane. Pass **Kiln Fm.** and at the Garsington road, **Blenheim,** cross (CARE) into the residential road opposite. At the shops, go left into a narrow, climbing bridleway path.

4. At the road turn left, north, for 250 m. Where the road bends right to Wheatley, turn left into a green lane which leads to a bridleway crossing two fields diagonally right. At the brook (bridge), follow the left hedge for two fields to the road.

5. At **Horspath** turn left on the road for 200 m, under the disused railway bridge (CARE), and at the Green, cross right (CARE) into Manor Farm Road and then Spring Lane. Turn left into Blenheim Road, which deteriorates into a rough BOAT track rising up to **Horspath Common**. At the "T" junction (**Resr.**), turn right (*once the Oxford to London coach road)* and enter the Lodge gates on the left, into **Shotover Park.** The bridleway, initially a wide avenue of magnificent trees, leads down, northeast then east, to the A40, where the dual carriageway with fast traffic indicates a

Route **21**:-ROBIN's Ride to roman DORCHESTER

SPINNING ALONG.

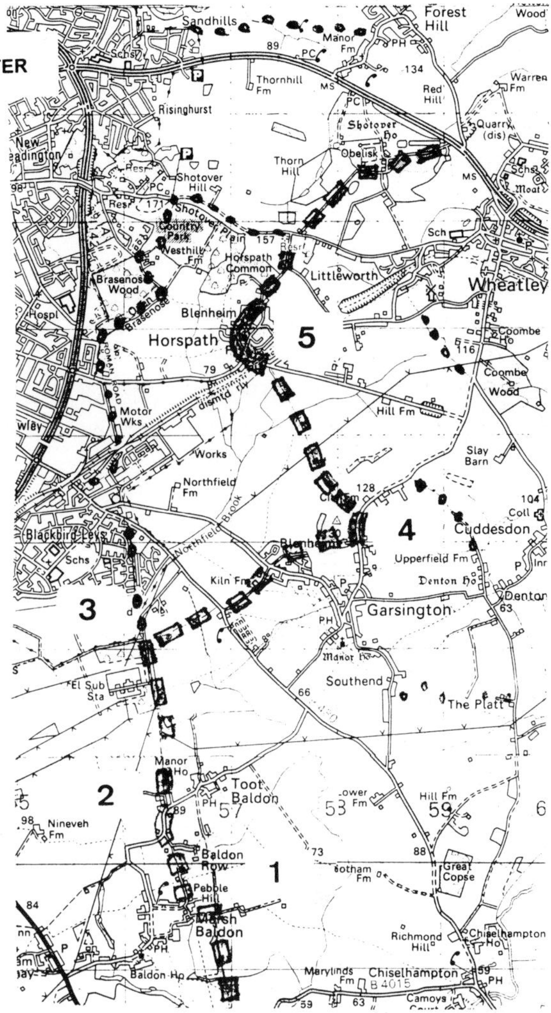

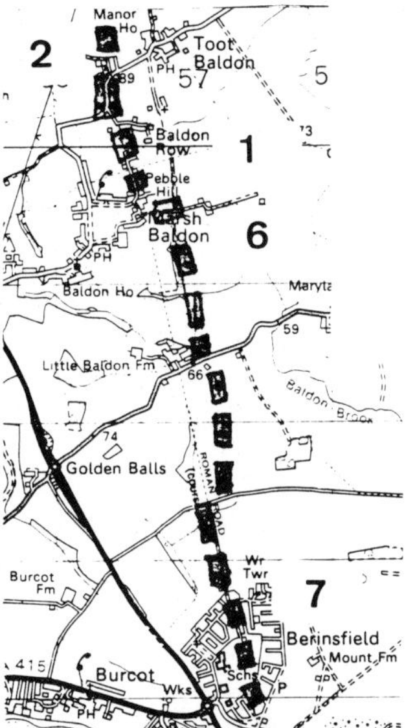

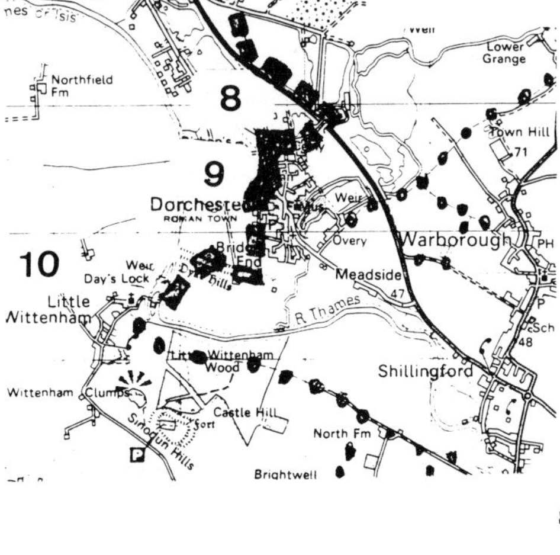

Reproduced from the Ordnance Survey 1:50,000 map with the permission of The Controller of Her Majesty's Stationery Office © Crown copyright (85436M).

FAIR AND FORTY.

point of return. *(The large, and largely unaltered, landscape gardens in front of the 18 C House, now the home of Lt. Col. Sir John Miller, formerly Crown Equerry to the Queen, were completed in 1730. They contain ornamental temples, a rectangular lake, and specimen trees. His grandmother, concerned by drunkenness among the quarrymen at* ***Wheatley,*** *donated a temperance hotel, "The Merry Bells", later a library & village hall*

6. Southwards from **Marsh Baldon.** From the southeast corner of the Green, take the farm track east for 200 m and turn right on a bridleway alongside a wood going south (parallel to, but east of, the Roman road). After the cottages at **Little Baldon Fm**., cross the B4015 (CARE) onto the field bridleway opposite. At a farm track junction, turn right and then left, to rejoin the original line of the Roman road into **Berinsfield** (*a village, built on a wartime airfield and named after St. Birinus, the first Bishop of Dorchester, who baptised King Cynegils of Wessex in AD.635).*

7. Continue due south, beside the playing field and go straight on through the housing, (or turn left round the outer peripheral road). At a "T" road-junction, cross (CARE) into the bridleway spinney opposite. At the A423(T), bear left on a good bridlepath between the wide, coppiced road verge and an ex-gravel pit (*now a lake used for aquatic sports*). Take the equestrian bridge over the A243(T) and continue past the cricket field to the cross roads (GR.576948).

8. Turn left into **Dorchester** (*where Birinus was granted land for his first church by the two Saxon kings he baptised. The Augustinian Abbey, founded around 1140, was destroyed by Henry VIII except for the church and a guest house which in 1652 became the grammar school and more recently, a small* ***Museum****).*

9. Turn first right, at the war memorial, into Watling Lane, a narrow back road. At a bend opposite the allotments, take the public bridleway on your right signposted to "*Day's Lock*". Initially very narrow behind a cottage garden, the path soon emerges into open fields going due south to the **Dyke Hills**. Turn right on a narrow track leading to a field at **Days Lock.**

10. Go diagonally left across the field to a gated, metal bridge over the Thames below the prominant landmark of **Whittenham Clumps** and Sinodun Hillfort. (Robin Cleminson continued south to the Ridgeway and then east along the South Downs to Newhaven).

[Alternative continuation]

Continue down High Street, **Dorchester** which is now without heavy through traffic. *("The George" PH, one of two fine 15 C coaching inns. has a gallery & an external staircase whilst the "White Hart" tel. 01865 340074 has a large coaching yard and quiet garden behind).* Cross the long, curving stone bridge over the River Thame, before it joins the River Thames 1 mile downstream, and then turn first left into the hamlet of **Overy**. Continue north east, via a field bridleway and an equestrian bridge under the A423(T). This offers two possible links with the Chiltern Hills, using Route No. 20 and going either (a) via Berrick Salome, Hollandtide Bottom, to Brightwell Baldwin and Pyrton, or (b) via Roke and Ewelme, to the combined Swan's Way, Ridgeway & Icknield Way.[1]

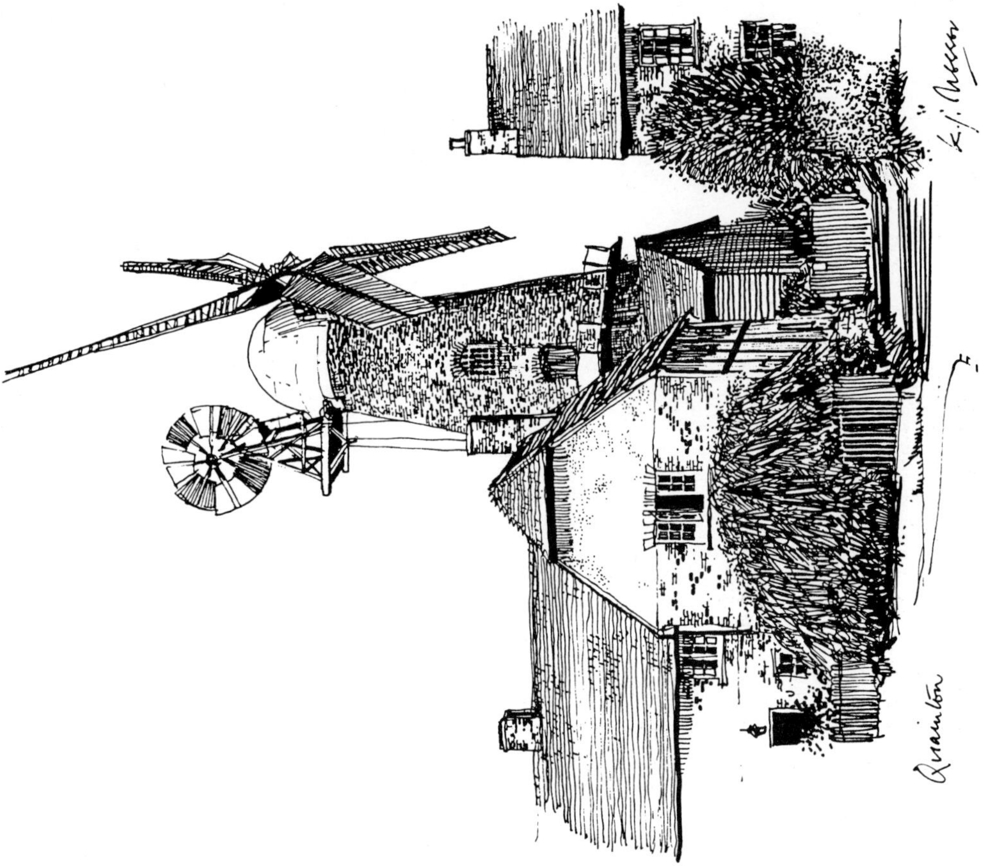
Quainton

Route **22:-WAYLANDS WAY - 1**

Map 1 - Quainton to Twyford

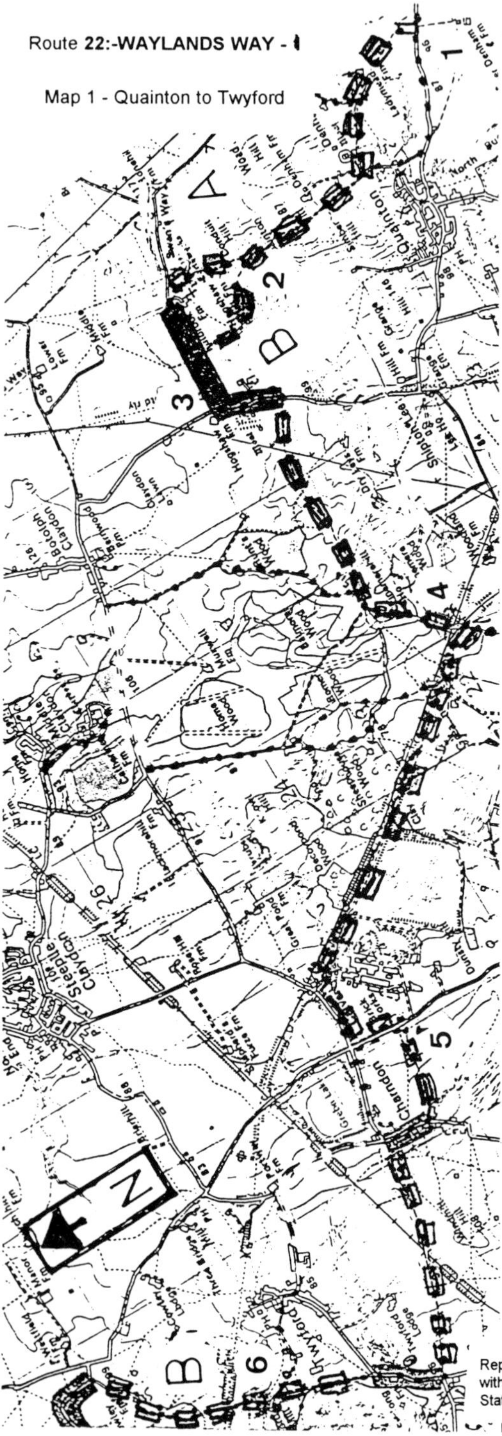

Map 2 - Twyford to Cottisford

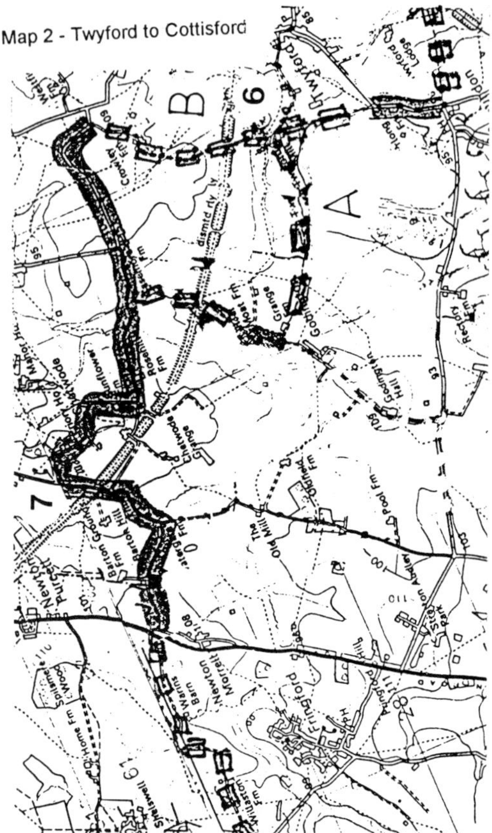

WAYLANDS WAY -Section I   Route 22

88 miles, linear

Ordnance Survey maps:-

Landranger 152, 151 , 163, 164, 165, 174
Pathfinder 1045, 1070, 1068, 1069, 1070, 1091, 1115, 1135, 1154

Length:

88 miles (141 km) in total, of which
56 miles (89km) bridleway/byway.

Parking & starting point.
Starting from **Quainton** 2 miles north of Waddesdon on the A41(T).

(i) Mrs. Grete Ricketts, Banner Hill Farm, Quainton, Bucks HP22 4AQ (tel. 01296 75543) (GR.761194). Riders' B&B at "*The White Hart*" PH Quainton.

Parking & finishing point.

(i) Mrs. Sylvia Cox, Sower Hill Farm, Woolstone, SN7 7QH. Uffington, Oxon (tel. 01367 820758)

(ii) "The White Horse" PH Woolstone, Uffington, Oxon SN7 7QL. Riders B&B Horses B&B can be arranged (tel. 01367 820726)
(iii) Mrs. Rugge-Price, Stainswick Manor, Bourton, Shrivenham, Wilts SN6 8LD, (tel. 01793 784133; mobile 0850 916604).

"***Waylands Way***" is a long-distance route between Quainton, Bucks. and Waylands Smithy in the Vale of White Horse; going via Cherwell & West Oxfordshire Districts. Because of road traffic on the A43 road to Northampton at Ardley (Junction 10, M40) and on the bridge over the Thames at Lechlade, it is divided into three separate sections as follows:-

I Quainton to Cottisford,
II Cottisford to Lechlade,
III Lechlade to Waylands Smithy.

The route is here described from north to south, but it can be followed in the opposite direction. It can also be extended from Waylands Smithy eastwards along the Ridgeway, then north along the "Swans' Way" to form a circular route.

Route description

1. At **Quainton** (*the village which was recorded in the D. B. as the "Queen's place", has a 15 C Market Cross, a windmill and 17 C almshouses),* take the bridleway from Banner Hill Fm. northeast then north across fields to **Ladymead Fm.** where a track leads northwest past **Denham Lodge** *(a 17 C moated manor house*) and then turns due north to rise steeply up to the top of **Quainton Hill** (mast and viewpoint, 187 m alt). Continue north over rolling pasture land to **Conduit Hill.**

2. <u>Choose either 2(A) or 2(B)</u>

2(A) Drop steeply down through fields to the right of 17 C **Fulbrook Fm.**, with team jumps and medieval village earthworks on the **Swan's Way**, here a gated metalled road.

2(B) Turn north west through a gate and go down left to **Hogshaw Hill Fm.**, still out of sight, and join the road further west, avoiding two road gates. Turn left along the road.

3. At **Hogshaw Fm.** "T" road-junction, turn left and ride south along the road (CARE). After 600 m enter the field bridleway on your right which follows the hedge north-northwest up to a ridge (138 m alt) and goes due west on alternate sides of the hedge to the farm buildings at Finemere Hill. Turn southwest along the track to **Finemere Hill Ho.** (*a timber & brick house reputedly built for single*

mothers by Florence Nightingale, when she lived at ***Claydon House*** *nearby, after she had introduced reforms in army catering, sanitation & medical practices in the Crimean War and then founded in 1860 the first school for professional nurses. Claydon House, itself, has "the most perfect expression of Rococco decoration in England" with wood-carved rooms in Chinese & Gothick style.).* Take a field bridleway by a pond into a wood, both being BBONT. sites and drop down to a track going southwest, over a railway level crossing and then a railway bridge.

4. Enter the gate on your right into a field bridleway and go north west to exit onto a track at another bridge by **Greatmoor Fm**. Continue northwest on a field bridleway then in a spinney for 2 miles to **Calvert**. (*The London Brick Company demolished the prominent Nine Chimneys in July 1995 and the claypit is now used for railborne waste*). Follow the segregated bridleway through the gantry crane operations to the site road entrance. After 100 m turn left behind the houses into a wooded bridleway going west. At the cross-roads, turn left still inside the wood and then inside a field for 500 m. (*This is a new bridleway dedicated by the LBC although not yet shown on OS maps*).

5. After a ditchbridge, cross the road to an excellent hunt gate and bridge into a field bridleway going west to **Charndon**. From the Valley Farm track (some buildings are due for redevelopment), turn north along the road for 400 m and at a "T" road-junction turn left into a field bridleway. Some sections of this 1.4 mile bridleway are heavy self-firing clays especially over the railbridge; they require CARE and PATIENCE when wet or dry. At the **Poundon** "T" road-junction, turn right north for 600 m. along the Twyford road. Leave the road after **Red Furlong Farm** and continue NNE on a BOAT to **Twyford Mill** (*race yard for jumpers*).

6. <u>Choose either 6(A) or 6(B)</u>.

6(A) Turn west, before the Mill, between the covered manege and the stables, then past the all-weather racing track along a field bridleway curving northwest to **Grange Fm., Godington**. Turn right on the road for 200 m to a gated bridleway at **Moat Farm** onto a farm track leading past a private church and under a disused rail bridge to the Chetwode road. Turn left.

6(B) Continue towards the Mill but turn right, fording the millstream into a sunken lane bridleway (impassable in winter floods) leading north over a disused rail bridge and across fields to **Cowley Farm.** Turn left west on a minor winding road to the hamlet of **Chetwode**.

7. After **Sunflower Farm and Priory Ho**., **Chetwode** turn left at the "T" road-junction, southwest towards **Stratton Audley**, over first a disused railway and then a stream at the **Watergate Farm** "T" road-junction. Turn right along the road (verges) to the O.C.C boundary at **Newton Morrell**. (The by-passed road to the left gives bridleway access to Newton Morrell Farm livery stables and saddlers Peter Ray tel.01280 848048). Cross the A.421 (CARE) onto a BOAT leading west past **Warin's Barn** and **Willaston Farm** *(earthworks to the south indicate the site of the medieval village*). Exit onto the minor road from Fringford to Cottisford. *(You are now in Flora Thompson's "Larkrise to Candleford" country).*

8. <u>Choose either 8(A) or 8(B)</u>

8(A) Go straight over, down the road to **Hethe** (*stream, and "Whitmore Arms" PH tel. 01869 277654*). Bear right through the village and after the Church yard and **Tangley Fm,** enter a field bridleway on your right through wooden gates of the well-kept Tusmore Estate. Follow a green lane and field hedge to the northwest corner of **Fox Covert.** Turn left southwest onto a BOAT.

8(B) Turn right along the road (verge) to **Cottisford**, bear left at the road fork and then turn left to the Church and Cottisford House. At College Farm, where the road bends right, take the BOAT on your left going southwest past **Fox Covert**.

9. Follow the BOAT track along a field hedge into a plantation. About 150 m before the track ends at a road, a field bridleway from **Hardwick** crosses from the left. Turn right into a bridleway under a broad glade of yewtrees leading northwest to Tusmore Parkland. At the end of the glade, the bridleway forks (*ahead along an avenue of chestnuts is* **Tusmore House**). Turn left to double gates and ride west for 400 m along a macadamed estate road, and over a stream to gates on your right where the bridleway crosses parkland to the south of the House and enters a green track, "Sheep Walk", going to **Park Fm**. Beyond the farm buildings is the very busy A43.

The first section of Waylands Way terminates here. *(The Dept. of Transport proposes to upgrade the A43 to dual carriageway with a road bridge, including an equestrian parapet, over the A43 to allow local traffic to cross into Tower Road. Work was due to begin in 1996)*.[1]

53

La bataille fait rage.
The battle is raging.
Die Schlacht tobt.

Route 23:- WAYLANDS WAY - II

Map 3 - Fritwell to Sandford St. Martin

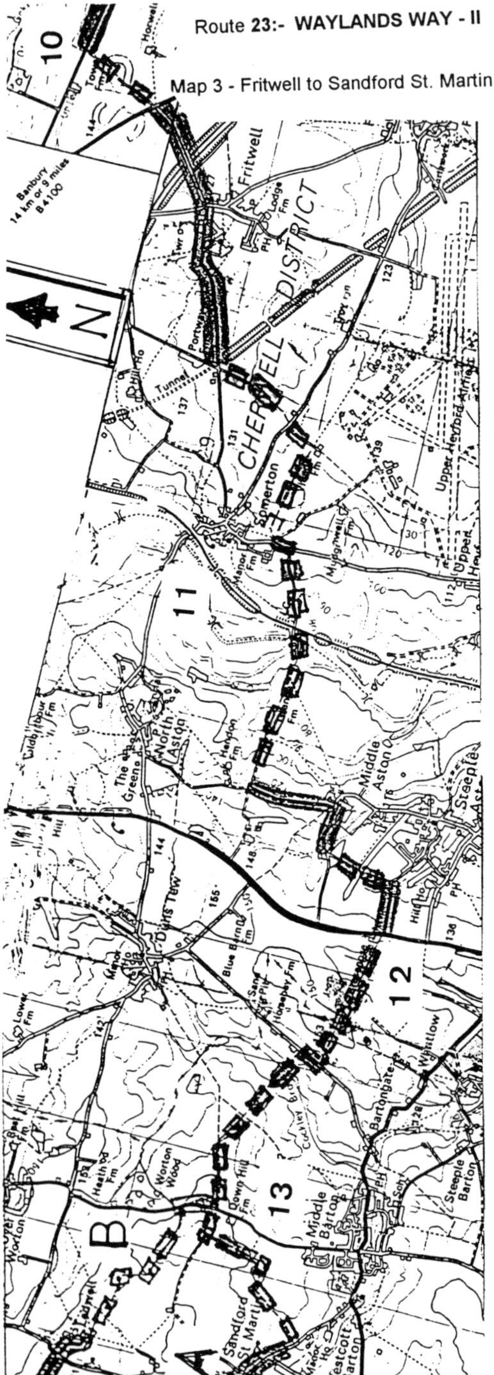

Map 4 - Sandford St. Martin to Stonesfield)

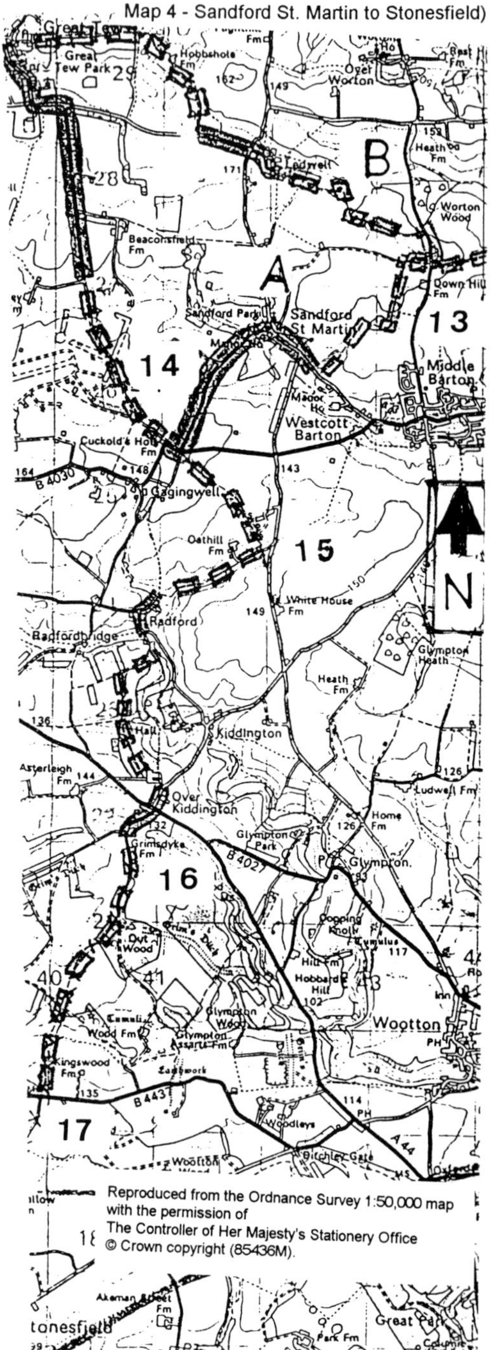

Continuing from Cottisford (from the west side of the A43 opposite Park Fm.).

10. Continue west along Tower road for 1 mile and, one field before **Tower Fm,** turn left onto a bridleway going south into a green lane. Cross the B4100 (CARE) onto a road opposite going over the M40 into **Fritwell**. At the cross-roads, continue west past the Church and the Manor House to **Portway Fm**. Turn left onto green lane bridleway going south into a field, and cross over the minor road (Somerton to Ardley) to **Village Fm.** buildings at the corner of the former **Upper Heyford Airfield** (flying now discontinued). Turn right before the sawmill fence along a field-edge bridleway (beware of rabbit holes) going west to **Somerton**.

11. At the road opposite **Manor Fm**, turn left along the road for 200 m to a farm track bridleway leading right, westwards, to a level railcrossing. (CARE Use the BR telephones before and after crossing this Inter City line). Go west over the Oxford Canal, bear left to go over the River Cherwell and enter a spinney along a raised dyke. Enter a field bridleway to **Grange Fm** and follow the farm road (verges) to the North Aston road. Turn south along the road to **Middle Aston** and turn right at the "T" road-junction. After passing a newly-landscaped garden with lake, turn left into a woodland bridleway going south to **Steeple Aston.** Turn right along the road up to the A423 (Oxford to Banbury). Cross (CARE) onto the bridleway opposite at **Brasenose Fm**.

12. Go due west along a bridleway for three fields to a minor road (Middle Barton to Duns Tew), turn right (verge) north for one field and then left onto a farmtrack bridleway before **Horsehay Fm**. Cross **Cockley Brook** (GR.452267) and on rising ground ride northwest on a field-edge bridleway through a hedge with a crossing bridleway (coming south from Duns Tew to Middle Barton). Continue north west traversing across the next field to a field-edge bridleway track (coming from **Duns Tew)**. Turn left west along the track to a minor road just north of **Down Hill Fm**. Turn right along the road.

13. Choose 13(A) or 13(B).

13(A) Turn left almost immediately along a farm track bridleway for 150 m, turning left off the track at the first field. Go due south on a field edge bridleway for two fields, west for one field, then south again for two fields to a minor road. Turn right into **Sandford St. Martin** village and then fork left at the memorial before the church. Go down to the stream along a minor road (verge) up to the B4030 near **Cuckold's Holt Fm** (GR.411254).

13(B) Continue by road past High Ley and Heath Cottage Farm to **Worton Wood.** Take the field bridleway on your left (GR.435275) for four fields along the south side of Worton Wood. Cross diagonally northwest to the inner corner of an "L" shaped field and after two more fields enter a lane into **Ledwell** (*OE. word meaning " loud spring or well*"). Bear left to the cross roads and take the road opposite to Great Tew & Little Tew for 500 m, then turn right, down a farmtrack bridleway going north. Keep **Hobbshole Farm** on your right (GR.411291) and immediately below the farm buildings find a bridleway track which contours left, west. The field-edge bridleway leads,

Somerton

below a walled woodland park to a gated path, at the back of the "*Falkland Arms*" PH on the village green of **Great Tew**. Turn right, then left on the road above the school and ride past the Church to rejoin the Little Tew to Ledwell road. Bear left and take the first road on the right (GR.401287) signed "Beaconsfield Fm". Go due south for 1.7 km where the road becomes a bridleway track. Ford the River Dorn at Poor Bridge.and on rising ground go south then southeast to a spinney. Turn left to **Cuckold's Holt Fm** (GR.410256).

14. At the "T" road-junction sign-posted **Sandford St. Martin,** cross over the B4030 (CARE) into a field bridleway opposite via double farm gates. Turn southeast, follow the left hand hedge for one field, then right hand hedges for two fields to a spinney behind the Bennetton factory dropping down to a brook.

15. Turn right along the concrete farm track to **Oathill Fm**, entering the field bridleway which follows the brook through a field and spinney into **Radford** hamlet. Turn first left, by a barnyard furniture unit, south down to Radford Mill. Go between the mill pond and millhouse to wooden stables and a hunt gate. The bridleway rises, first left across the field, then right along the top hedge, to a gate in the corner of the next field giving access to the plateau above. Follow the left hand hedge due south, through a farm gate into the park land above **Kiddington Hall** (*and Lake in grounds designed by Capability Brown*). Follow the farm track to the farm, go between the cattle sheds (awkward gates) and farm buildings. Exit right onto a minor road at Park Fm. **Over Kiddington** (GR.411223).

16. Turn right for 250 m, cross the A44 (CARE) into a minor road leading to Ditchley. Turn left to **Grimsdyke Fm** where the farm track goes due south, along a spinney, to a field bridleway going southwest on the west side of **Out Wood**, along a field hedge to a hunting gate. Bear left south south-west across the next field, down to a narrow spinney (a bridleway crosses at right angles). Drop steeply down the edge of **Kingswood** and cross the brook (ford & bridge). Turn right along Kingswood Bottom for 150 m then go left steeply up a greenlane, due south, to a "T" road-junction on the B4437 road to Charlbury.

17. Cross over (CARE) into the minor road opposite going south towards **Stonesfield**, but after 500 m turn sharply north-west into a field bridleway along the south side of **Sheer's Copse**. Jink left, after a farmhouse with paddocks and right again, along a field-edge BOAT to the B4437.

18. Cross over the B4437 into a green lane and ride north west for 4 miles on a gateless BOAT, continuing as a farm track past **Dustfield Fm** and the Lodge gates of **Ditchley Park**. (*This estate acres with an 18 C model farm and mansion was designed by James Gibbs, used in WW2 as Churchill's weekend HQ and is now an Anglo-American conference centre).* Where the farm track forks after **Norman's Grove**, bear right (ie still north west) on a green lane. Cross the B4022 (CARE) and another minor road, continuing until the green lane becomes the Spelsbury to Chipping Norton road (GR.353236).

19. Take the bridleway on your right, north across one field to the hedgerow, where a bridleway comes from **Lidstone**. *(You are now enjoying high Cotswold views over the Evenlode valley. A 187 m alt. Trig. point is in the next field to Lidstone*). Turn sharply left in the same

field and go southwest, cross over the Spelsbury to Chipping Norton road (CARE) and continue on a cross-field bridleway down to a stone barn at the head of a valley of pinewoods. Follow the wooded track down to a stream and a spinney of poplar trees. Turn right across the stream, taking either of two short bridleways into the hamlet of **Dean** (the first goes back sharply right up a narrow, overgrown lane, the second goes up a field).

20. At the road, take the lane for 100 m to Dean Manor (*some fine drystone walling at the gateway)* opposite the field bridleway. Enter the bridleway in the paddock on your left, cross the brook and climb up one field to a lane into **Chadlington.**

21. Choose 21(A) or 21(B).

21(A) Continue west by road through the village, past **Chadlington** Church, over the **Westend** crossroads, down to **Brookend,** taking the first right into Cross's Lane. The road (good verge) climbs past **Blaythorne** back to 190 m alt. on the A361. Cross the A361 (CARE) into the field bridleway opposite, continue north west across a minor road, along a wood and then down the field into a narrow wooded valley. Turn left on a wooded bridleway down to **Sarsden** lake. (GR.293227) (*A late 17 C mansion in a park landscaped by Humphrey Repton*).

21(B) Turn right at **Chadlington** church into Church Lane, turn left at the bowling green, and then right at the "T" road-junction to **Millend.** At the childrens' playground, turn left down to "*The Tite*" PH *(the name means "spring"; the car park is lower down).* Continue by road for 1.5 miles to the A361. Cross (CARE) onto a large semi-circle verge with stone walls and pillars marking the tree-lined approach road to **Sarsden**. Where the road forks after 500 m, take the bridleway straight ahead along a new estate drive until this latter contours right into parkland. Continue on the bridleway down the wooded valley to **Sarsden** lake.

22. Turn left onto a bridleway lane going south though **Fairgreen Fm.** and becoming a field-edge bridleway rising to an avenue of trees above **Merriscourt Fm** *(twin stone pillars and a belevedere seat were erected by Lord Moreton).* Cross two fields to a lefthand hedge which joins a bridleway track on high ground (GR.295212 at 180 malt) just before the main road and ***Lyneham Barrow & Seetlement***.

23. Turn right on a farmtrack bridleway down to **Lyneham.** Cross straight over the minor road by the mansarded facade of Lyneham Farm and follow the road round the hamlet to the farm track going west past Priory Farm, under the railway and towards **Heath Fm**.

24. Turn right north onto a field bridleway leading to the woods and the parkland of **Bruern Abbey** *(a 12 C Cistercian abbey, an 18 C mansion and now a school).* Turn left along the road for 500 m. Where it bends south to Milton- and Shipton-under Wychwood, take a field bridleway going southwest to the south-east corner of **Herberts Heath** on your right. The bridleway bears left into a long, narrow piece of marshy common land which rises along Common Lane into **Fifield** village (*where for several centuries the villagers made sheep hurdles from the Bruern Abbey coppice woods*).

25. Choose 25(A) or 25(B).

25(A) Continue over the crossroads by road uphill to the A424 or

25(B) Turn left at the crossroads for 200 m and join a field bridleway going right

Map 5 - Stonesfield to Chadlington

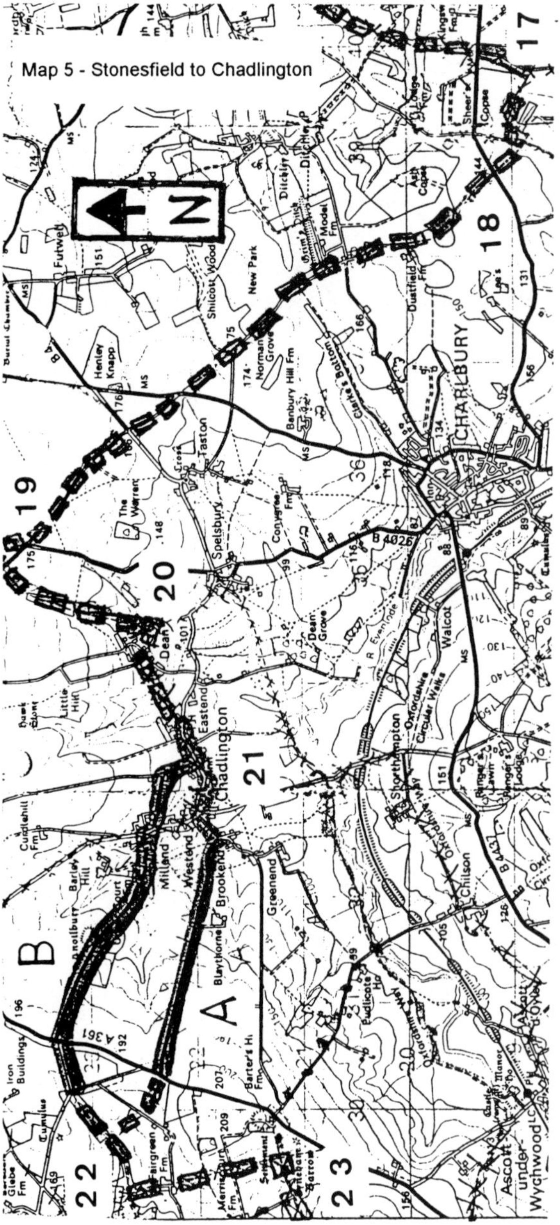

Route 23:- WAYLANDS WAY - II

Map 6 - Chadlington to Fifield

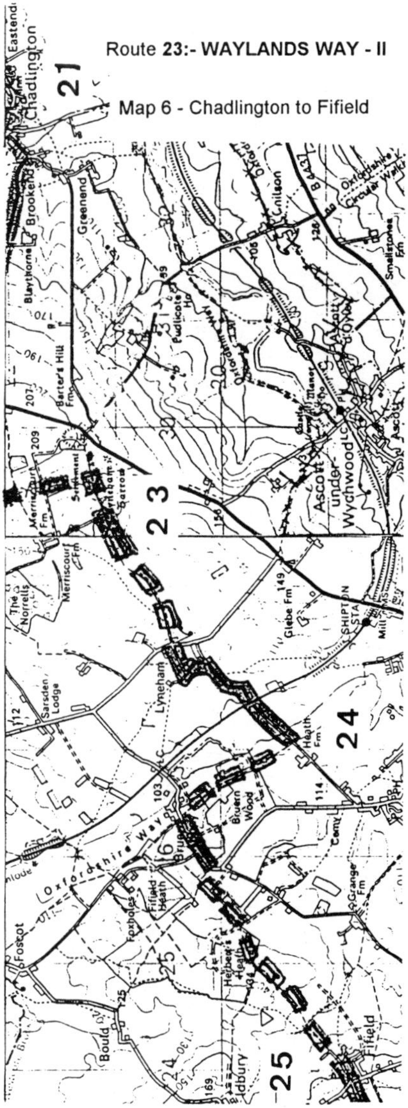

Route **23:-WAYLANDS WAY - ii**

Map 7 - Fifield to the Barringtons

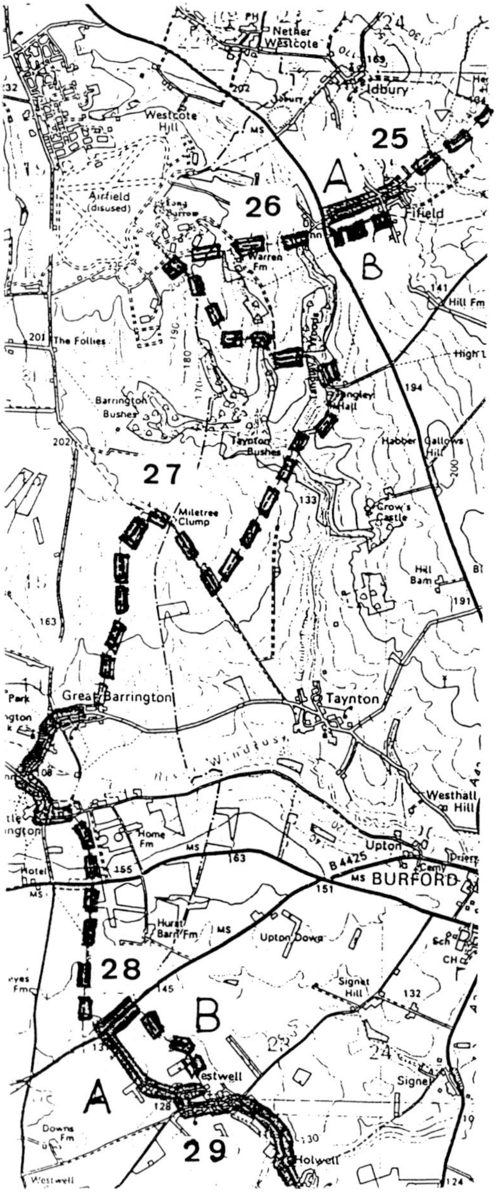

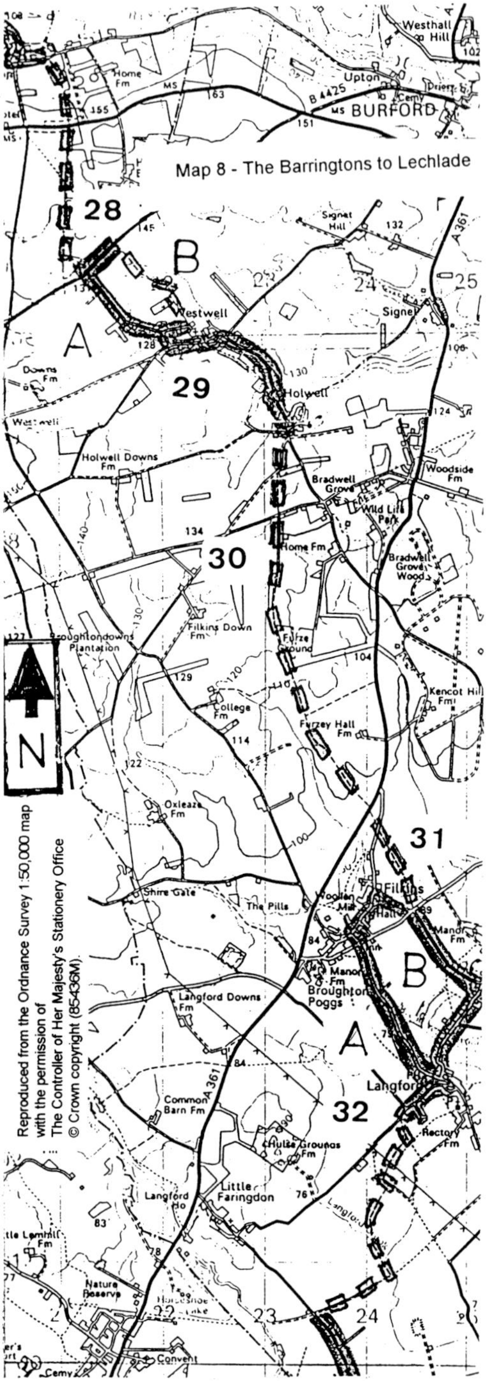

Reproduced from the Ordnance Survey 1:50,000 map
with the permission of
The Controller of Her Majesty's Stationery Office

across three fields to the A424. Turn right for 200 m along the verge. Cross the A424 (CARE, fast traffic).

26. Go down the wooded track below ."*The Merrymouth*" PH on a ridge running at 200 m alt. between the Oxfordshire and Goucester Cotswolds. Then climb due west on a green lane past **Warren Fm** into open fields on a level with disused **Rissington** airfield. At the last hangar, turn sharply left southeast along the hedges of three fields and then due east down over a stone bridge to a ruined barn. Rise diagonally up the field to a green lane which goes east and bends down as a wooded track to Tangley Farm and cottages. Turn right into a park above **Tangley Hall** (small and beautiful in Cotswold stone and apparent abandon). The bridleway follows two field edges then goes west steeply down to a bridge across Coombe Brook, then turns sharp left south west again to climb steeply up through **Taynton Bushes**. Follow the edge of four fields southwest to a bridleway junction, turn right going northwest past a barn to the end of **Miletree Clump**.

27. Turn south along the edge of five fields dropping down to **Great Barrington** village. (*On the hillside to the east are the medieval open quarries of* ***Taynton*** *which provided stone for Windsor Castle, St. Pauls, Blenheim and most of the Oxford colleges).* At Great Barrington Farm; first go right round the barn, then left to the road and then right again along the road. At the Memorial, fork second left, past **Barrington Deer Park**, with its Palladian House and church, down to the **River Windrush** (*"The Fox" PH has a yard for horses separate from the carpark & garden*). Continue by road to **Little Barrington** and at the top of the broad green (formerly a quarry) turn second left, Middle Road, for 300 m. Take the field bridleway opposite the church and ride uphill to the A40. Cross (CARE) onto the bridleway track opposite going due south past a stone barn to a pine plantation. Cross a narrow field to a road bend and a "T" road-junction on the A433 (Burford to Bibury) and exit onto the road (CARE).

28. Choose either 28(A) or 28(B).

28(A). Take the minor road opposite for 1 km to a "T" road junction, or

28(B). Turn left along the A433 for 400 m to a small wood "The Beeches" and take the fieldedge bridleway on your right going down south east for two fields. Turn right along the hedgerow up to a wood. Turn southeast again to paddocks, and turn right along a wide farm track to join the road and go left to a "T" road junction.

29. At the "T" road-junction, turn left through the village of **Westwell**. Ride past the church, the rectory, Manor House and village green with duckpond and a stone monolith *(This war memorial, inset with "I", is a relic from the magnificent 13 C Cloth Hall at Ypres, a city totally destroyed by artillery in the Passchendaele trench battles of WW1).* Bear right and continue southeast by road to **Holwell** village. At the village cross, follow the road right and after the detached house (formerly a school), fork right along a farm track bridleway going due south. After one field, the track bears off south west; whereas you fork left at a gated spinney to enter a field bridleway going due south to a minor road.*(This was the Roman Akeman Street. The* ***Cotswold Wildlife Park*** *is 1 km along the road to your left, in 200 acres of* ***Bradwell Grove****, a 19 C Tudor-style mansion).*

Thames at Lechlade

30. Cross into the gravelled lane opposite, which becomes, in turn, a green lane, then a field edge bridleway along **Furze Ground** woods. Follow field hedges going due south for 2 km. Near **Furzey Hall Fm** (one field away to your left at GR.239061) the ride goes south east as a field-crossing bridleway for 1 km to the A361 (good visibity & verge). Cross (CARE) onto the bridleway opposite for one field, then directly over a minor road into a green lane which leads to a field bridleway (CARE ! rabbit holes).

31. Choose31(A) or 31(B).

31(A) Turn right along the road verge for 30 m, then turn sharp right to **Filkins Hall** and left into the village. *(The working **Woollen Mill** houses a tea shop and an exhibition of traditional Cotswold Woollen Weavers & other crafts. The stone quarry-work museum is named after George Swinford, estate foreman to Sir Stafford Cripps. Several cottages have large vertical stone slabs as garden walls*). At *"The Lamb" PH* turn left, cross the busy road (CARE) into the road opposite for 1 km to **Langford**.

31(B) Cross the busy road (CARE) into the minor road opposite to **Broadwell** (1 km). At the "T" road-junction, turn right along the road to Langford. (*Langford church is a particularly splendid example of early medieval cruciform architecture and art, with high arches under the tower, and two fine carvings in the south porch, one Saxon, the other 14 C).*

32. In **Langford** village, turn right along the road towards Little Faringdon. After the last building, a school, turn left through a farm gate onto a field bridleway going south along the left hedge for two fields. Enter double gates ahead and turn at right angles south west along the right hedge of one field. Enter the next field (by an old barn), turn left for 100 m then turn right again, southwest, along the left hedge to a gate into a ridge-and-furrow pasture field. Turn southwest and find diagonally left a hunting gate and wooden bridge over **Langford Brook**. Turn left and follow the brook south to a gate giving access onto a disused railway embankment. Go southwest to a minor road and turn left along the road for 1 km to a "T" road-junction on the B4449.

33. At the "T" road-junction, turn right. (**Kelmscot** *village, signposted to your left, is where William Morris lived for 25 years until his death in 1896 in the Elizabethen Manor, now owned by the Society of Antiquaries and containing furnishings, wallpapers, fabrics and pictures by him, Rossetti and Burne-Jones*). Go past **Paradise Fm.** and Leaze Farm to A417 road junction, where **"***The Trout Inn*" PH with car, caravan and boat parking lies on the **River Thames** by **St John's Bridge** (*and the highest lock on the river*).

This terminates the second section of Waylands Way. The BHS Oxfordshire Committee hoped in the early 1990s to negotiate for "permissive" bridleways, via Kelmscott and an island in the Thames, to the Lechlade road opposite **Buscot Park** (NT). This route is currently a public footpath.

The crossing of St. John's Bridge, over the river and lock, is for experienced riders and horses only. Turn left along the A417 for 100 m (CARE) and ride over the bridge, (DEFENSIVELY occupying the left half of the short, narrow bridge). Traffic has to slow down because of the road bends. Turn immediately right into a wide field entrance with double gates.[1]

Route **24:-WAYLANDS WAY - III**

Map 9 - Lechlade to Coleshill

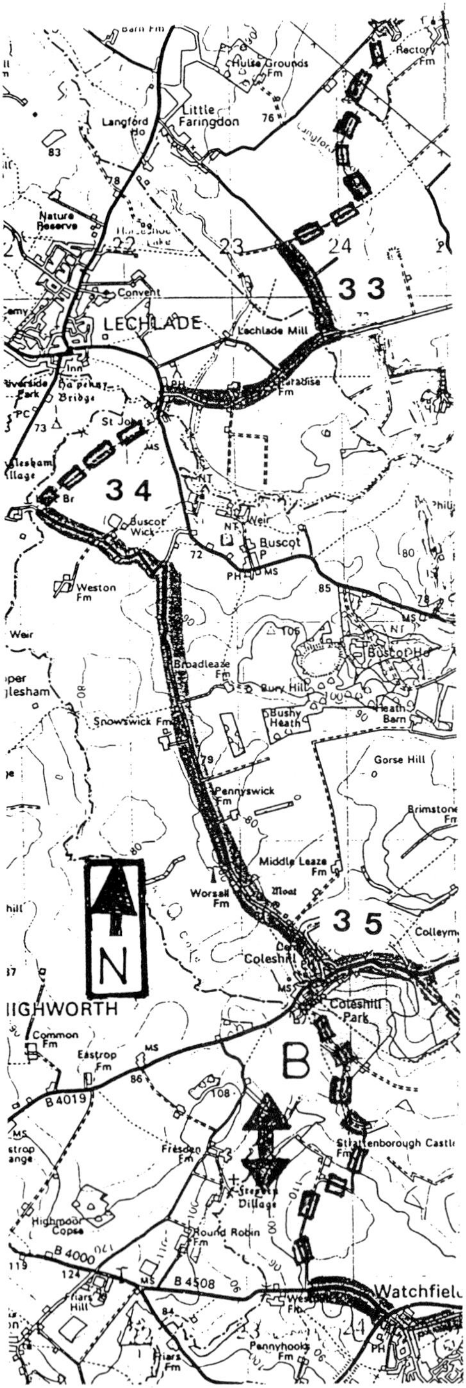

Map 10 - Coleshill to the Smithy

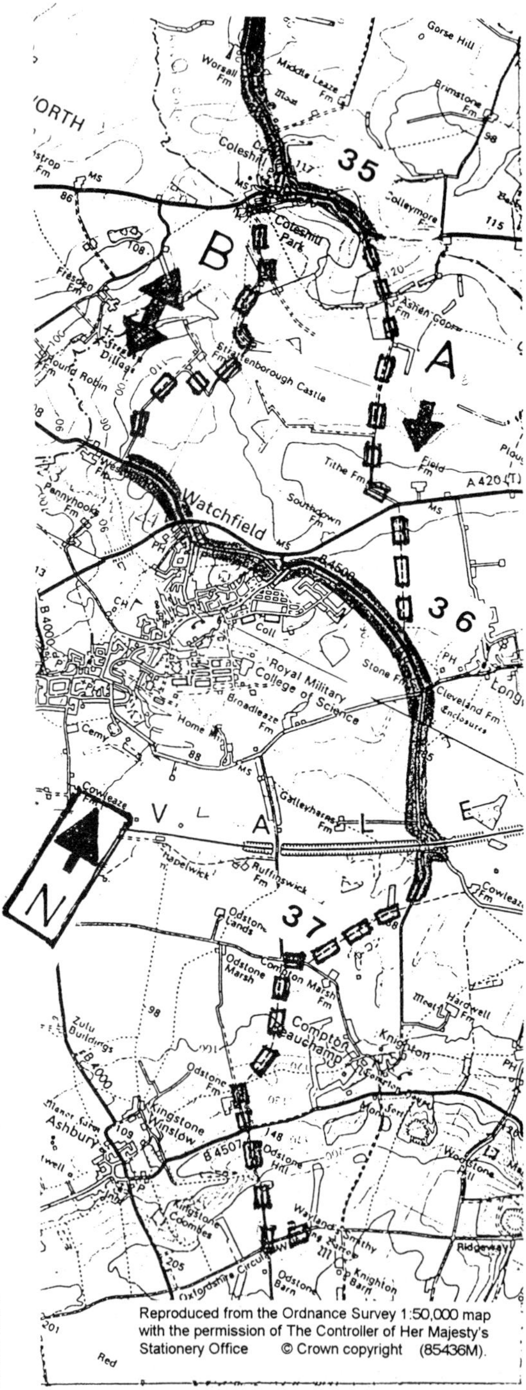

Continuing from Lechlade (from the south side of St. John's Bridge).

34. Turn immediately right into a wide field entrance, with double & single gates, onto a BOAT going southwest across four fields to **Lynt Bridge.** Turn left along the road, past **Buscot Wick** and **Weston Fms.** to the "T" road-junction. Turn right along Snowswick Lane for 2 km to **Coleshill**.

35. Choose 35(A) only if southbound

35(A) Bear left at the road fork, then turn left along the B4019 (verges) past **Coleshill Park** and woods. (GR.246938). Take the bridleway farm track via **Ashen Copse Fm.** to **Tithe Fm.** on the very busy A420 (Oxford to Swindon road). The Southbound, crossing demands CARE and PATIENCE. There is good visibility in a waiting area on this convex side of a road bend. (*Crossing in the opposite direction is NOT recommended. Northbound, the route crosses the A420 at Watchfield about 2 km west)*. Enter the field-edge bridleway opposite, which becomes a green lane, to the junction with the B4508 (GR.267906).

35 (B) If going north to Coleshill. At Point 36, continue northwest along the B4508 to **Watchfield** past the green lane bridleway. Turn first left, then first right along the new road to the Shrivenham Hundreds Industrial Estate. At the "T" road-junction, turn right to wooden railings marking the wide verge of the A420 (GR.243906). Cross (CARE) into the road opposite (the B4508 to Highworth). After 800 m, but before the road goes downhill, turn off right on a farm track going north to Watchfield Common Wood (Nature Reserve) and **Strattenborough Castle Fm**. Turn right 150 m . before the castellated buildings. Find a mid-field bridleway dropping down, due north to Waterloo lodge in a wooded copse. Follow the bridleway track round left into the parkland and exit right into **Coleshill.** Turn right then left above Coleshill (*NT*) estate buildings, cross the B4019 (CARE) to the Church and village green with stone cross. Turn right along the road *(The PH has a hitching rail in the carpark*) and turn left along Snowswick Lane.

36. Turn left along the B4508 towards **Longcott** for 450m to the crossroads at **Stone Fm**. Go straight over into the minor road opposite towards Uffington. Go under the railway bridge and turn right along the road to **Compton Beauchamp** for 500 m. Take the field bridleway on your right going south-west towards **Compton Marsh Fm.** (*The Vale of the White Horse is here only 90 . above sea level*). Turn right along the minor road for 200 m to a "T" road-junction.

37. Enter the gate on your left into a field bridleway which follows the hedge south-south-east and then south-south-west as it rises up to **Odstone Fm.** Turn left by the white cottages into a lane which leads up to the B4507. Cross over onto the concrete track opposite and climb up the steep escarpment to a wood (*200 m alt.*) and a rewarding view over the Thames valley and the Cotswolds hills. Continue on the farm track for 500 m. At the **Ridgeway** here a BOAT, turn left for 300 m to **Waylands Smithy** in the clump of trees to your left. *(The Long Barrow burial mound is unfortunately approachable only on Shank's Pony).*[1]

Waylands Smithy